THE
FEARLESS EXPERIMENT

Jenell —
I can't wait to
hear your story —
However you choose to
tell it.

Lindsay

LINDSAY McPHAIL

DEDICATION

To C.J. my best friend and lover of all things adventurous, you have awakened me to the fearless spark in me that can never be extinguished. You have my whole heart for my whole life.

To my wonder boys, Sawyer, Thatcher, Crew and Charlie you make me want to be a better person, and sometimes you make me want more wine.
But mostly the better person thing.
I love you more than life!

To my mommy who has always told me I could be anything I wanted to be. You make me brave and I love you!

And to the rest of my amazing family, who has courageously and patiently endured this experiment.
I love your guts.

CONTENTS

FOREWORD

Writing a book is like giving birth.

Ironic isn't it ... a man-comparing book writing to birth-giving? What do I really know about giving birth! The notion isn't much different than me, as a man, trying to write a compelling foreword to a book that speaks to a woman's soul. I hesitated at first when Lindsay asked me—thinking it's a bit out-of-the-box; which, by the way, I won't use to describe Lindsay's type—for she'd likely resist being put in the box outside the box.

So here I am, wondering what I might say as a man to lead you into the life-changing read of The Fearless Experiment. So, if you happen to be just browsing through this book wondering if you'd be interested—trust me when I say—it's well worth the read.

I have 'given birth' to three published books. As a result of the first one, One Small Sparrow, a unique youth-based charity organization called Sparrow Clubs USA (www.sparrowclubs.org) was founded-- empowering kids to help kids in medical crisis. Since 1995 we have adopted nearly a thousand children in medical crisis to schools and youth groups across twenty-seven states as Sparrow projects. My book and the whole idea of this charity was based on my personal experience which Lindsay writes about in Chapter One of her book.

In the spring of 2002, I was introduced to CJ and Lindsay McPhail when they were youth pastors at Table Rock Fellowship in Medford, Oregon. The Sparrow Clubs organization and program was in its infancy— unknown, undeveloped, unprecedented and seriously under-funded. My background was being a PE teacher and football coach, with no business being a founder and director of a public charity. But it's funny how God seems to put His people in such places where we, and others, think we have no business being. I had to take a leap of faith from my stable career to pursue this passion in my heart.

Something deeply resonated within CJ and Lindsay when they first heard my story. They jumped at the opportunity for their youth group to get involved with Sparrow Clubs. Three-hundred-plus kids en masse soon met and adopted a local boy who needed a bone marrow transplant, whose family was struggling and needed help. God showed up in that Sparrow project. Soon after, CJ and Lindsey got a call from 'you know Who' — which for them required a huge leap of faith as well..

During the previous few summers the young couple led small groups of middle and high school students on mission trips to Mexico. After the Sparrow project they were inspired with a vision of how God could use them, and Sparrow Clubs, to bring the mission trip to Medford and share God's love in practical ways to thousands of unreached students in local public schools. CJ and Lindsay threw caution to the wind and pursued the call in their hearts to launch Sparrow Clubs first chapter outside of our small office in Bend, Oregon. God used CJ and Lindsay to accomplish amazing things for and through Sparrow Clubs for six years — and it still thrives after their departure. I will always be indebted to them for their experiment of trusting God beyond their fears.

As a writer, the birth process metaphor makes sense to me. It is the conception, development, labor and delivery of my voice in book form. It is a painfully long process, pregnant with hopes and dreams — that someday, somehow, this 'child' of mine will have an impact in the world, or even in one life. Nothing compares to the arrival of that 'child'; it is truly part of you. To know your voice and have your voice known is a labor of love. Your voice can only come from the authentic you. And finding it inspires others to find their own.

As a reader, Lindsay's voice speaks clearly, honestly and compellingly through The Fearless Experiment. Her '{FIGHTING WORDS}' throughout invite us to reflect on God's Voice—the Author Who speaks our true identity into our existence and awareness. Her stories challenge us to encounter God with faith in action, too. Her voice is engaging; ringing true to a love that can conquer any fear.

Happy birthday and hooray to your voice in The Fearless Experiment, Lindsay! As a guy writing the foreword to a book meant for women, I'm coming out of my man-closet for this one as a fan of Lindsay McPhail, woman's book writer. Her words resonate in my soul. I believe they will in yours too.

Jeff Leeland
Author of *One Small Sparrow*, *Disarming The Teenage Heart*, and *A Thousand Small Sparrows*.
Founder of Sparrow Clubs USA

INTRODUCTION: FLYING SQUIRRELS

There is no sofa, table, bookshelf, or refrigerator that is safe from my third son Crew's acrobatic abilities. I call him my flying squirrel. One of his favorite tricks is to stand on something and jump to you...whether you're looking or not. He has no fear, and it's scary. I am always pulling him off of things because his fearlessness gets him into trouble; he breaks things, hurts others, and usually proudly carries a badge of honor (aka bruise, scrape, or bump) from his latest conquest.

I, on the other hand, am no flying squirrel. In fact, I have spent the majority of my life hiding behind all of the things I thought I wasn't. I started *The Fearless Experiment Blog* in 2011 as a way to conquer the fear that kept me from living the life God designed me to live. I asked readers to join me, and it's been an amazing journey so far. What I've realized though, is that there's more to being fearless than meets the eye. Fearlessly following Jesus is awesome and noble in many aspects, but if it's not bursting with God's love and purpose it can break things, hurt others, and leave us with many unnecessary battle scars.

This book is for those who hunger for God and wonder if there is something more. This book is for anyone who has ever backed away from a dream too scary to utter out loud but too amazing to let slip through the cracks of an ordinary life. This book is for everyone ready to get messy in love and in life so you might have eyes to see and ears to hear the abundance God has in store for you…right now!

One more thing, through out these pages you'll come across little extras, don't skip them. "Fighting Words" will appear frequently and are simply Scriptures that have really impacted me. It's tempting to skim them, especially the ones you've read a million times but I challenge you to dive in. Look them up and read them in their full context, maybe even in a different translation of the bible than you usually use and ask God to show you something new. There are also an abundance of questions. Answer them. Answering questions honestly is foundational in realizing God has already given us most of the answers we're looking for. O.K., let's do this thang!

ONE: AN EXTREME STORY

On September 6, 2011 a knock came that changed our lives forever and proved that God was at work in a mighty way. As I opened the door to Ty Pennington and the Extreme Makeover crew, I took a step into a future God is still astounding me with.

That change really started years earlier. It started with an unlikely hero whose life was cut short but whose destiny would change the lives of tens of thousands.

Dameon was a 325-pound seventh grader. He was teased and bullied. He was isolated and alone— until Jeff Leeland (one of my personal heroes) came into his life. Jeff was a teacher, and more than that he was Dameon's friend. For one period a day, Dameon had someone who loved and accepted him for the beautiful creation God had made him to be. So when Dameon found out that Jeff's baby son, Michael, had been diagnosed with cancer, and his insurance company wouldn't cover the bone marrow transplant the baby needed to save his life, Dameon took action.

From a boy nobody expected to be great came a gift that has transformed thousands of lives — including my own. Dameon emptied his bank account of his entire life savings: sixty dollars. He took that money to school, gave it to Jeff, and said, "Mr. Leeland, you're my partner, and if your son's in trouble I want to help him out."

Of course, like any of us would do, Jeff refused Dameon's money and thanked him. But when Dameon wouldn't take no for an answer, Jeff finally gave in and accepted the gift with tears in his eyes. Dameon's gift sparked something throughout the school, and in eight weeks, a student-led campaign raised $228,000 and paid for the transplant that saved Michael's life.

From that overwhelming gift, Jeff started Sparrow Clubs USA. Sparrow Clubs is kids helping kids in medical need. It challenges schools to adopt local children with medical or developmental conditions and through sponsored community service hours, the school raises funds for children who need them. (Go to www.sparrowclubs.org for more info.)

While Dameon and his sacrificial gift sparked an amazing organization, Jeff is the unsung hero of this story in my mind. He accepted Dameon's gift even though his pride told him not to. He accepted Dameon's gift knowing $60 wouldn't make any sort of dent in the $180,000 he needed to save his son's life. He accepted the gift not knowing the tidal wave of blessing and inspiration it would create.

Jeff's ability to accept a $60 gift changed my life profoundly. In 2002, my husband C.J. and I joined Jeff at Sparrow Clubs and started a chapter of the organization in Southern Oregon where we live. We were honored to be a part of so many families who were fighting for their children, and seeing the students fight along side of them was life altering. We worked for Sparrow Clubs for six years before we decided to branch out and start a business of our own, following dreams God had laid on my husband years before.

Unfortunately (and fortunately) 2008 was not the best year to start a business in a developing industry, and we lost everything. EVERYTHING! Only a few months before my 30th birthday, with three kids in tow, we had to move home to live with my parents. Jobless and still reeling from our oldest two sons being diagnosed with autism, hope seemed far, far away. I remember saying out loud that I was sure God was trying to destroy us. Not my brightest moment, but the feeling was real.

Months and months and months passed with no income, and the grinding debt we were incurring from living on our credit cards was suffocating. Wait! I promise this gets better. You won't need Prozac to finish our story. It was through these months of not knowing how to feed our family, not having a home or jobs, and having to admit failure that we grew closer to God than I ever knew possible.

During this time, our oldest son Sawyer was "adopted" as a Sparrow at a local middle school as a way to spread awareness about autism. That was humbling to say the least, but it was also significant to experience the "other side" of Sparrow Clubs. We had to learn how to accept time and resources from other people. We had to die to our pride and honestly learn to accept our son's autism—all for the very first time since his diagnosis—and it changed us.

In 2011, after C.J. found a job and we were starting to get our lives back on track, we were nominated to receive a home from ABC's TV show *Extreme Makeover: Home Edition*. We dreamed about what could happen if we were chosen, but were sternly brought back to reality whenever we watched an episode of a deserving family who had received a home because they'd saved lives of people in developing countries or had adopted twenty kids with special needs. That wasn't us. We were just a normal family struggling to come back from utter destruction. My husband worked for a local hospital, and as the mom of young boys, I pretty much spent my days wiping butts and snotty noses. Throughout the entire nomination process we said, "If this happens, it is 1000% God because we don't fit in with the other 'Extreme' families."

On the morning of the knock at our door, our family was huddled in my oldest son's tiny room wondering if we would be chosen to receive a gift so huge it could only come through an act of God.

After the sound of knocking stopped, we heard a familiar voice; we opened the door to Ty Pennington shouting, "Good Morning, McPhail family!"

Before the greeting ended, I was already weeping with joy. It was a gift of grace birthed from years of struggle, heartache, and gut wrenching humility.

As we moved forward into that gift, we knew that knock on our door wasn't a happy ending; it was an outrageous beginning to a story God is still writing.

What would it look like for you to wake up to *your* outrageous beginning? What would it be like to live completely free from everything that binds you? Free from insecurity, pride, unbelief, unforgiveness, or jealousy? What kind of life would you have if fear wasn't a factor and the word "impossible" seemed more like a dare than a declaration?

Ready to find out?

Welcome to The Fearless Experiment!

TWO: THE POVERTY OF UNIQUENESS

"The pressures of religious conformity and political correctness in our culture bring us face to face with what Johannes Metz calls *'the poverty of uniqueness'*"
                    –Brennan Manning, Abba's Child

Have you ever run from your quirky uniqueness? Have you ever ignored really incredible parts of who you are because they seemed different than the people you look up to? That, my friend, is the *'poverty of uniqueness'* longing to be someone we're not all the while missing out on everything we truly are.

|FIGHTING WORDS|: Obviously, I'm not trying to win the approval of people, but of God. If pleasing people were my goal, I would not be Christ's servant. Dear brothers and sisters, I want you to understand that the gospel message I preach is not based on mere human reasoning. I received my message from no human source,

and no one taught me. Instead, I received it by direct revelation from Jesus Christ. (Galatians 1:10-12 NLT)

Autism has brought so many curve balls to our family. Years after our oldest son's diagnosis and another diagnosis for our second born, I am still fighting daily to embrace acceptance. Deep down sometimes I just want my kids to fit in. I don't want them to have to experience the teasing or tears that go along with ignorance and bullying. I don't want them to stand out anymore than they already do. I want them to be safe and feel loved. Embarrassingly, for me, there are days I long for them to be just like everybody else.

Several years ago, our fence blew down in a raging windstorm. The guy who came to fix it was huge, at least 6'6 and over 300 pounds. He had a scruffy beard and wasn't overly friendly. When he knocked on the door, I opened it just wide enough to stick my head out—not because I was afraid of him, but because I had a 100-pound Bernese Mountain dog and three boys who run for an open door like prisoners on a jailbreak.

While the repairman stood outside, I stood blocking the door, explaining about the fence while simultaneously using my body to keep the wild beasts from escaping. That lasted for all of thirty seconds before Sawyer (my oldest), squeezed between my legs and made it onto the front porch. I should mention that Sawyer has always been GIGANTIC for his age. Oh, and my kids are almost never dressed...*ever*...they hate clothes. Anyway, Sawyer squeezed out wearing only a pull-up. (Even though he was four then, he looked about six.)

Sawyer ran up to the big, scary, fence guy, wrapped his arms around him and said, "I've missed you."

The guy didn't know what to do and awkwardly patted Sawyer on the shoulder and said, "Thanks."

One of the best things about Sawyer is his ability to just love people. His joy is contagious, and his passion for life resembles that of a Labrador puppy. A very big Labrador puppy.

I can think of a hundred funny stories to share about my quirky guys, my boys are amazing...AMAZING! Each account starts with my children doing something outrageous and at times embarrassing, and too many of them end with me shushing, stifling, and shutting them down. It's almost like I can feel the "what ifs." My fears become palpable, and the anxiety over what truth might slip out of their tiny, unfiltered mouths keeps me one step ahead of them, rarely allowing them to really just be themselves. That's hard to admit, and even harder to write, just in case you were wondering.

All of my "wonder" boys have given me so much

perspective and taught me to find joy in every little victory. They have made me a better person and challenged me to dig deeper with God. It's only been recently that I've been able to embrace their special little selves and all of God's Glory they carry. It took me years to realize they have the raw authenticity that so many of us hunger for but are too prideful or self-conscious to actually own.

In being able to value their candid uniqueness, I've realized my only job is to push them to shine. The other day, Sawyer looked at me and said, "Mom, my Autism is really a gift, it's the greatest thing about me." What insight from a nine-year old: to see something that has been hugely challenging, not for what it takes from us, but for what it has added to our family.

I don't think God causes illness, but I have watched my special boys discover and display so much of God's beauty, that I often wonder if they simply have a unique, authentic, and cut-to-the-chase way of experiencing the divine through something society finds uncomfortable. What if we all started to value the unsightly, rough edges of our character as beauty in the making? What if we didn't hide behind the strengths we want people to see, but allowed God to rise and shine in the glorious uniqueness that sometimes looks like weakness? We would cease to just read the words on the pages of our Bibles, and we really would be *new creations in Christ*. Not defined or held back by who we think we're not, but pushed forward to blaze because of all God is and all He has done inside of us.

We were created to be more than mediocre copies of each other. When we're held back from being our true selves because of what others might think, we live in a prison of sorts. Uniquely and thoughtfully, each of us was knit together to be different, beautiful, brave, earth shakers. God created so much abundance, fulfillment, and adventure, and we miss out on it all when we just try to fit in. Getting to the edge of uncomfortable but never jumping off into the vastness of the distinctive life He has for us keeps us safe and ordinary, it also keeps us from what we were made for.

FEARLESS has been the battle cry of my guts for a couple of years. Not because I *am* fearless, but because I long to be. As our family stepped into the new life God had for us after the EMHE build, the new soundtrack to my life was a resounding drum beat, like the one you hear in the movies as warriors go into battle. THUMP, THUMP, THUMP. God continued to put challenges in front of me, and the thumping just got louder and more intense. God was beginning to open my eyes to the fierce warrior and leader He created me to be, which came as a bit of a shock since I had always avoided all things uncomfortable.

Have you ever noticed how so many of the things we say we *would never...could never do...*He births in our lives—if we let Him? It's pitty (as in makes your pits sweat) and squidgy and awkward, but so very freeing!

Being brave enough to embrace our unique selves isn't just a good idea; it's what God expects from us. To be secure enough to own our stories of redemption, pocked by hurt and struggle, and then to being brave enough to tell those same stories is a war plan so powerful not even satan himself can contain it.

{No Time for Echoes}

|*FIGHTING WORDS*|: *For the Lord is the Spirit, and wherever the Spirit of the Lord is, there is freedom* (2 Corinthians 3:17 NLT).

I can feel a season of God raising up fearless women around the world. Just looking at the women in my own circle, I am in awe. God is drawing them out, asking them to join His work in loving others, and calling them to serve in the most outrageous ways.

My friend Kim is the kind of person who just does stuff. She doesn't wait for permission to help others. She doesn't need the bolster of likes on Facebook to move. She just hears God and moves—even when it's scary, even when it costs, even when she questions why God would choose her. For years she and her family spent Sunday mornings feeding the homeless in a local park. Rain or shine, freezing or sweltering, she went out and loved on hundreds of the overlooked and undervalued in our community.

Not too long ago, I was setting up for a Fight Night *(a monthly night of worship and teaching I lead in room above a bar)*, and Kim came up to me with an almost uncontainable joy and whispered, "I'm going to a club up north this weekend."

I was knee deep in an ocean of tangled sound equipment and distracted by the throngs of women coming up the stairs as we scrambled to be ready for that night's event. I started to give her an, "Oh that's awesome" response, keeping it fake and surface.

Then what she said sunk in. I turned toward her, "Wait...what club?", I dropped everything as she told me she was researching Strip Church *(an organization that equips women to reach out to those in the sex industry)* and realized there wasn't a huge outreach presence for our local strip club. She had found the nearest hub and was driving four hours north to jump in feet first and get some training. She was glowing and radiant, and I knew this passionate woman was about to do something life altering!

As weeks went by, she and I continued the conversation of what an outreach of this sort would look like in our valley. She was looking for other women who loved God and wanted to share His love with women who had been judged, disrespected, and overlooked for far too long. I told her I would continue to pray for her and support her, but couldn't commit to actually *doing* anything because my plate was too full.

That night I was taking a bath thinking about what God really wanted me to do. I was thinking about love and how I had been asking God to help me experience it in a new, real way for months. He made it clear to me that night that I had a choice; to live out love by saying "yes" to His invitation to work with Kim, or I could continue to just echo words about love I've heard from people I admire and read in books.

I realized right there I had become an echo. I had been feeling God pushing me toward a new kind of authentic love, but I had been hiding behind my "busy" schedule. I had filled my life to the brim with good things but not necessarily things God had asked me to say "yes" to.

On a side note: It's amazing how we can use being busy with good things as a defense against the big, scary, greater things God has called us to. I wonder how many monstrous, seemingly impossible dreams God has put in front of us excitedly, hoping we'll dive into with Him, only for us to say, "I'm just too busy." Hiding behind the words "I'm too busy to…"

keeps us feeling just important enough to say "no" to the life we were actually created for.

When Kim approached me, I loved what she was about to do, but I was scared OUT OF MY MIND! I asked myself what I could ever offer any of these women, and I was full of great excuses *not* to take the risk and just love.

I knew I had to say "yes." On the night of the first outreach, Kim and I met under a bridge close to the club. It was Valentine's Day, and we decided to take roses to the girls at the strip club, along with a note introducing ourselves. As we sat in my car under the overpass that night we prayed through Micah 2:13 and asked God to break through any barriers, physical or spiritual. We asked for the courage to take those last few steps into the very visible club that sits on the corner of Main Street in our small town. As we prayed, a tangible peace came over us. But I have to admit, when we entered the doors, I was a bumbling idiot who had forgotten how to form actual words. Still, I was in awe as I watched my beautiful friend, Kim, do what she was made to do. Not save, not preach, not even pray…but LOVE. And so a new journey to love outside the box, outside of religion, outside the camp began (Hebrews 13)—a journey I almost missed out on by choosing to be an echo.

I know God is still transforming me — a middle-aged mother of four — into something fiercely and strangely beautiful. It's scary, but with each passing day a Braveheart-esque battle song is being composed inside of my head.

God is creating your inner sound track right now too. Can you hear it? If the fearless soundtrack is resounding drums, God is asking to add a bag pipes to the score...these loud, sweet-but-slightly awkward notes will now accompany the thunderous thumps of the drums, encouraging us on as we step into the unknown and often uncomfortable adventure of knowing who we are so we can change the world, or maybe just impact one life.

No matter what the tone of your battle cry is, it is a wake-up call to stop just consuming, and to really allow the Holy Spirit to invade every area of your life. Whether our musical score is the *Rocky* soundtrack or one of those relaxing nature CDs, one thing is clear: we need to stop trying to please people, even good people. We need to stop trying to live up to the expectations of others and society and even "Christian" culture and DARE to follow God and what He is asking us to do. This daring starts with owning who you are created to be!

We can hear the most amazing teachings, do incredible studies, and read powerful books, but if we're not actually out there, putting love into action, we're really just echoes of someone else's story. It's time! It's time to be creative, curious, and adventurous! You have a unique voice; let God build *your* battle cry. It's time to move into His wake-up call… FEARLESSLY.

STOP right now and take some time to write down what He's saying to you about the sound track He's writing in your life.

{I Only Paint the Toes that Show}

|FIGHTING WORDS|: *So now there is no condemnation for those who belong to Christ Jesus. And because you belong to him, the power of the life-giving Spirit has freed you from the power of sin that leads to death* (Romans 8:1-2 NLT).

I only paint the toes that show on any given day. From a distance, it looks like I have a decent pedi going—and I do mean a distance. But if you look up close, you would see about seventeen layers of gunky, chipped "You don't know Jacques" OPI polish on my toes. The big toe on my left foot is still swollen and throbbing from an unfortunate forking (which is why forks don't belong on the floor, FYI). And the calluses on my heels? Well it's just not proper to talk about them in mixed company, or in *any* company for that matter.

Anyway, why am I going on about my disgusting man-feet? Because I think they kind of represent who

I am in life: how I try to portray myself so others will think that I have it together. Not *all* together because that would be annoying, but just together. What I want you to see is that I have four crazy boys, two with special needs, and although we have been faced with many challenges, I am strong, and I am easy going, and I know what I'm doing. *That's what I want you to see*, and that's probably what it looks like from a distance. But when you get even remotely close enough you will see that on a lot of days, I am just wiped out. I use humor and put myself down to guard against your judgment, and I have no clue what I'm doing or how to be a good mom to such complex boys.

I'm sick of pretending to be someone I'm not. I will never be the super June Cleaver homeschool mom who has all of her ducks in a row. Guess what? I'm a horrible housekeeper; I have seven junk drawers...IN MY KITCHEN! The craziness that is my home is not just because my kids destroy everything (and they do) but because I have too much going on, and cleaning is my *very* last priority. If you come to my house without any notice, my house will not be clean. EVER. And unfortunately for my husband, I've gotten to be really OK with that.

While some people hide behind a wall of false perfection, I find myself hiding behind a wall of calculated imperfection. I have always thought that if I can tell you enough of the bad stuff about myself up front, you will only see the imperfect parts of me I *want* to be exposed. It seems raw and real, but it's not — and weirdly it's my defense mechanism. It's as bad as manufactured perfection because it's creating an illusion distracting you from the parts of me I think are the weakest: the parts of me I think you'll see that will make you decide you won't like me anymore. Only as I've started to own all of who I am have I been able to stop hiding behind the labels I've given myself, and allow God to take me deeper.

There is something incredible about the fact that He can take the extremely under-qualified (me, you, those 12 guys back in the day) and turn us into extraordinary creations, set up to shake the foundations of the earth. It's easy to believe the bad, but it takes a little extra gumption to also believe the great about ourselves.

Why is it so hard to say "I am Uh-mazing!"? "I am bold, I am a leader, I am courageous and compassionate!"

God made us this way…so why is it so hard for us to own? Honestly for me, it's because I'm afraid you won't agree, so I act on the response I'm assuming you'll have over the truth that God has whispered in my ear.

All through the New Testament it says: "Whatever you ask in My name, I will do it"(John 14:13 HCSB).

"Nothing is impossible with Christ"(Luke 1:37 NLT), "I can do all things through Christ" (Philippians 4:13 NIV). THIS IS OUR REALITY! When we choose to believe in our own strength or when we choose to believe we are defined by our shortcomings, we're forgoing everything He promises us. We're choosing to read these words in the Bible and believe they must be for someone else, and we miss the point of it all.

Everything great that has ever happened in my life has taken place when I've been vulnerably and noticeably under qualified. I went to Chile to serve and didn't speak a lick of Spanish, and while I was there God cured me of an eating disorder I'd had for a decade. I got married before I had a clue about what love really is or about how to respect another human being, and through the muck and years of challenges, I've found my best friend and someone who continually calls out my good. I had my first baby four weeks early, and though I thought I knew everything. I knew NOTHING. Sawyer has undone everything I thought I knew about life and love, and being a mother has taken me deeper and made me a better person. We moved four hours north to Portland, OR because God called us so we just went: house unsold, future unknown. That turned out to be the most gut wrenching three years of our lives, but God used them to take us deeper and draw us closer to Him. We left a paying job to follow a dream in a new industry in a down economy. Uh-hem, *that* decision didn't end so well, but there's something about not knowing how to feed your family that yields a spiritual depth that almost feels like drowning...but we didn't drown. God just took us deeper. We moved back in to my childhood home with nothing, no money, no job, and no home of our own. Just a broken little family praying for a miracle. Then, against all odds, we were nominated for a little contest, and even though we didn't fit the bill, we were chosen to receive the most monstrously generous gift a community could build. It was a gift we didn't deserve, but through receiving it, we heard God whispering, "This is just the beginning. Don't you see? I work wonders in your weakness. Let me in and see what else I have for you. Let me take you deeper still."

It's taken years of heartache, challenges, victories, and encounters with God, but now in my mid-thirties, I am so grateful I can stand up and say: I love the person He is turning me into (gasp...can I say that?) I love that I can see a glimpse of what He's talking about in those verses I just mentioned. I love that I *can't* brag about these things because of anything I've accomplished, but because anything good in me is there only because He has turned my dirty laundry into something quirky, unique, and powerful.

Today is the day. TODAY is the day to start owning the great stuff about YOU. Today is the day to worship our Creator by being brave enough to love all of the great things He put inside of you and to start using them to love and build-up and encourage others!

| FIGHTING WORDS |: To each is given the manifestation of the Spirit for the common good. (1Corinthians 12:7 ESV).

WRITE IT DOWN. What are you good at? What is something unique and special about you? What piece of brokenness has he turned into gold in your life? Don't skip over this; it's not lame! Write it and read it and thank God for it. Then ask Him what He wants you to do with it!

{Naked & Exposed}
| FIGHTING WORDS |: Nothing in all creation is hidden from God. Everything is naked and exposed before his eyes, and he is the one to whom we are accountable. (Hebrews 4:13 NLT).

When I was in high school I worked at a bank. I have no clue how I got the job. I wasn't super great at math, and what I lacked in people skills I made up for with almost no common sense. Needless to say my time as a teller was short lived, but it didn't end without a chance to utterly humiliate myself...*on camera.*

I need to set the stage by telling you I am the middle of five kids. My parents always did the best they could to provide for us, but money was stretched tight, and we shared a lot. In the realm of things we shared (OK, so maybe "sharing" is a loose term for things I took without asking) were toothbrushes (OK, that wasn't a budget thing. I just always used whosever's was closest), clothes, and of course bras. I had my own bras, but my mom and older sister had better bras: Victoria's Secret bras. So I "shared" them *all* the time. They didn't fit perfectly but I didn't care. They were my favorite.

So back to the bank and ill-fitting bras. While I knew, generally speaking, that the bank was under surveillance, it never occurred to me that as a bank employee, I too was being filmed. It only became hugely, embarrassingly clear to me when, at a staff meeting one day, the bank manager announced to everyone that adjusting yourself whilst bending down behind the counter out of the customers view was NOT out of view of the bank VP who regularly reviewed the footage. SWEAT, GAG, PUKE! At that point my guts were in my throat, and I wanted to move out of the country, but if I left the room everyone else would know it was *me* the manager was talking about. My time at the bank began to flash before my eyes. Not only had I adjusted my bra a million times, but I was sure I had also tried to not so daintily pull borrowed underwear out of uncomfortable places, too. I don't think I had ever felt so naked, so exposed…so *humiliated*. Instead of giving up my intrusive habit of *"sharing"* undergarments, I left my job at the bank shortly after that meeting.

You know the mind-blowing, amazing thing about the difference between being exposed by God and being exposed by the world? Stripping off all of the lies and all of the barriers built out of pain before the Lord always results in breakthrough and growth. The beauty of spiritual nakedness is that it is never accompanied with guilt or shame or humiliation. It's the core of freedom and the birthplace of intimacy with our Creator.

We might see our "naked and exposed" selves as something to be ashamed of, but *He* sees us as He created us to be. I saw a pin on Pinterest the other day that said, "the enemy knows our name and calls us by our sin; God knows our sin and calls us by our name." When we think we can hide our flaws, when we spend our lives trying to be seen as perfect in the eyes of God and men, we are cheating ourselves out of the freedom and amazing grace that comes with being fully exposed.

In our humility and repentance we are transformed. In our deepest hurt and fears, we are healed and redeemed. What would it look like if you just made the decision to be naked and exposed? *Gasp!* "What will people think?" Well, it may not be easy, but inner revival and all things new, pure, raw, and real start with the courage to be exposed.

I can feel God crying out today: "You are not your failures. You are not your successes. You are not what you do. You are not your past. You are not your weight. You are not your looks. You are not your marital status. All that you are is in Me… ME! All that you are is because of Me. Today, *right now* you are complete in Me. You just have to see yourself through My eyes and My perspective: you are Mine, and that is enough."

Peter McHuen said in a conference once, "When you get to heaven, God isn't going to ask you why you weren't Moses. He's going to ask you why you weren't you."

{How We Are Vs. Who We Are}

|FIGHTING WORDS|: What actually took place is this: I tried keeping rules and working my head off to please God, and it didn't work. So I quit being a "law man" so that I could be God's man. Christ's life showed me how, and enabled me to do it. I identified myself completely with him. Indeed, I have been crucified with Christ. My ego is no longer central. It is no longer important that I appear righteous before you or have your good opinion, and I am no longer driven to impress God. Christ lives in me. The life you see me living is not "mine," but it is lived by faith in the Son of God, who loved me and gave himself for me. I am not going to go back on that. Is it not clear to you that to go back to that old rule-keeping, peer-pleasing religion would be an abandonment of everything personal and free in my relationship with God? I refuse to do that, to

repudiate God's grace. If a living relationship with God could come by rule-keeping, then Christ died unnecessarily. (Galatians 2:19-21 MSG).

When my oldest son Sawyer was eight, I homeschooled him because he was struggling and falling behind in school. One morning after he had a major meltdown, I realized how much emphasis we put on the connection between *what* we do and *who* we are. As Sawyer struggled that morning with simple math, I was rejoicing that my little man, who started the year not knowing his numbers, could actually go through the steps of borrowing in a two-digit subtraction problem. Sawyer has autism. Things that many of us take for granted and come easily to us are mountainous struggles for him. He was so weepy that morning as he focused on *not* being able to get the right answers. He kept saying, "I'm a failure. You're not proud of me, are you?" My heart broke as I realized he was equating what he does as who he is.

I can't even count the number of conversations I've had with women who have associated who they are with what they do...or don't do. The things that we're good at don't define us any more than the things we suck at doing. We can get lost searching for who we are and our purpose in life. We can get stuck and spin our wheels for so long, wondering what we're good at and what gifts we have, that we end up paralyzed because we feel unequipped and lost.

I know so many women who are gifted teachers or writers or athletes, who, when asked who God says they are, they answer with what they do and what they're good at. I've talked to women defending themselves and the walls they put up who say, *"well that's just who I am. ... "* Did I mention I was one of these girls?

For most of my life I've confused *how* I am with *who* I am. My friend Lu has taught me so much about the difference between how we say we are and who we really are. And how the two are really as different as night and day sometimes.

Lu is the founder of The Genesis Project: a powerful, 12-week program that unites emotional, spiritual, and physical health. A couple of years ago, as a successful gym owner, Lu felt like God was telling her to sell everything and move to Hawaii to be a staffer on a YWAM base. So she did. This girl has crazy powerful stories of how God has rocked her to the core. As a result, she's passionately in love with Jesus. Lu is a writer, speaker, coach and trainer. You can check out how amazing she is over at lucrenshaw.com. She is the first person to EVER give me a word from God. She told me He told her I had a prowess for leadership, and those words changed me. They opened my life to an awareness of and relationship with a God I realized I barely knew.

Lu is a "tell it like it is" type of girl. She's bold and beautiful and compassionate and full of grace, but she didn't always realize this about herself. In her own words, here is a snippet of her journey from being bound by a bit of an identity crisis.

> *The other day Lindsay and I had a conversation about how we are vs. who we are. As many of you know Lindsay will just tell you how it is...well so do I. So as you can see this could make for a very dangerous combination in a friendship...but it actually doesn't. It's like the Lord has laced my lips with some sort of grace, and that's what she hears. It's pretty weird actually. Even if it's straight up truth...I sort of sit prepared to hear a dial tone on the other end of the line, but I never do and it's the same for her.*

> *Not long ago I unbound the pages of my journals because I knew it was time to write the story of my journey out of who I thought I was. Some of the pages I came across made me cringe. They brought back so many memories of the woman I was, how I was. YUCK! Sure, there were good qualities about me but, oh dear Jesus, I was a mess.*

> *Let me just put "How I Was" in nutshell for you:*

Insecure, Inconsistent, Angry, Impatient, Unapproachable, Unavailable, Prideful, FULL OF SELF PITY, Perfectionist, Unkind, Ungracious, Bitter, Resentful...ok I'm just going to stop now, you get the point.

As time passed, I began to hear God's truth about who He created me to be. He gave me diamonds of truth about who I really am and I began to change. As He continued to speak to me, it started to open my eyes to HOW I WAS.

So back to my conversation with Lindsay, I was given liberty to speak into her life because I knew exactly where she was. You could hear the chains she was bound by, so basically I was like, "O.K. here we go." What came out were the bondages she had been walking in – we don't need to name em...hahaha. But the opening of the eyes to our strongholds gives the enemy less foothold. When we know the stronghold of sin we are walking in, we recognize it more clearly, joyfully repent, and then begin to walk in the opposite spirit. The opposite spirit is our original design. The places the enemy torments us the most, the things we think we will never be free of, the sin that haunts us; these are the places we are destined for the most greatness. You claim to be shy? I call bluff...God didn't make anyone shy; it's the enemy's silly little idea to keep you shut up for the rest of your life because what's actually behind those lips of yours could actually shift a culture. You're rebellious and it's just who you are? NO WAY, NO HOW! You are righteous at your very core. You will stand up for the things that others will not stand up for. You are riddled with righteousness and truth...but what if you started walking in it, raising your children in it? You are straightforward and rough around the edges? I think not. You are a dang teddy bear that's got more love and compassion shut away in your bones than you would ever care to admit. What would happen to your life and your relationships if those tough walls came down and compassion and love flowed forth? Crazy right?

My chains kept me from walking in relationship and from truly loving those around me. They kept my walls nice and high so no one would get in, so no one could hurt me....BAD IDEA! I am sitting here now, a woman radically changed, who can love, who can be loved, who has the heart of a momma, and who desires freedom for all the captives. What if I had never shed my own chains? Dear Lord...thank you for saving me.

When we take on Christ as our identity and shed the idea that *how* we are is *who* we are, it changes everything! We are a piece of Him, we are part of His parts, and that means we decide to be done with our agendas, our pasts, our failures, our pride, our walls and our control and let *who* He is overshadow *how* we are. He is love, He is power, He is boldness, He is wisdom, He is healing, He is forgiveness, He is not afraid; He is full of Joy and Peace and Patience. All of these things define who He is and what He does stems from those characteristics. So, when we slip Him on as our identity, these characteristics become who we are, they are how He sees us, and what we do stems from a place of intimately knowing Him.

Do you ever hide behind an illusion because it's just easier, because it feels safer, or because you're afraid of what your life will look like without the calculated persona you've been created?

If I ask you: "Who are you?" right now, how would you answer?

What parts of your past shade your answer?

Did your answer have anything to do with how *you are?*

Knowing that you're actually hidden in the glory of God, stop and ask Him how He sees you. What is the first positive *thought that pops into your mind?*

Ask Him to give you a verse that backs up what you just heard. Write it down and keep it with you.

PS. If you did this exercise and heard crickets, don't fret! God is speaking to you; you just have to tune into the right station to hear Him. Email me anytime and someone from my team will start praying with you!

Email: lindsay@fearlessexperiment.com

YOU ARE BEAUTIFUL.
YOU ARE SMART.
YOU ARE POWERFUL.
YOU ARE FULLY SEEN AND TRULY LOVED.
YOU ARE BOLD.
YOU ARE A WORLD CHANGER!

PRAY WITH ME: Lord help me believe those words. Help them change my life. I know you made me uniquely perfect for all of the dreams you have given me. Jesus, who do you say I am? Remind me of how much you love me and who you created me to be today!

THREE: UNDONE

{The Scariest Prayer I've Ever Prayed}
"Lord humble me" is by far the scariest prayer I've ever prayed, mostly because I never really knew what it meant to be humbled.

I get poison oak really badly about every other month. It doesn't help that our farm seems to be conveniently situated on Southern Oregon's largest patch of this vile weed. One or two times a year I have the added pleasure of rushing to urgent care because my oozing, itchy rash has gone from annoying to a dangerous allergic reaction. At least once a year, my eyes swell shut and I look like a monster for about a week. Years ago my yearly explosive reaction took place while working at an office job. This was before kids and before the thirty extra pounds said kids so generously helped me pack on. I was thin and full of energy and had a killer wardrobe. Usually, I looked pretty good. So when I showed up Monday morning looking like something out of a horror movie, my coworkers' reactions ranged from sympathetic to fearful. I was humiliated and I wanted to call in sick, but as part of a young couple struggling to survive on my minimum wage job and my husband's youth pastor salary, going home wasn't an option that day. So I went to the office — swollen and scabby. A guy who had never been overly friendly walked up to me and smirked. He must have thought this was his chance to put my overly spunky self in my place.

He came close and whispered into my ear: "We all have to be humbled at some point."

I've never been confident. It took me until I was twenty-one to recover from severe depression and an eating disorder that started when I was ten. There were times I longed to disappear, there were times when I felt like it would be easier to end it all than to take up any more useless space. For whatever reason, all of the emotion from years of such deep wounds flooded me the second his words were spoken over me. I could almost tangibly feel the darkness I had fought off for years start to cover me again. Was God doing this to me to put me in my place? Had my exodus from self-loathing been a good thing after all? Maybe I was starting to think too much of myself? I started to question everything. The enemy had twisted the thoughtless words of someone who meant absolutely nothing to me to reopen wounds I only thought were healed.

A few months later at our very last youth camp, while sitting around a campfire, my husband C.J. challenged our students to pray three words, "Lord, humble me." He said those three words could change everything. But I just pictured that day in the office and that coworker leaning over to whisper in my ear. Guilt, shame, and fear rose up within me. What had been meant as a simple challenge for our teens to surrender to God morphed into a turning point in my spiritual journey. God showed me the real meaning of that word and transformed all that I thought it meant into an image of freedom for me.

That night, as I lay under the stars, I whispered the prayer cautiously: "Lord, humble me." I spoke only three words, but what they symbolized was the release of a lifetime of shame, guilt, self-hatred, and doubt. All at once, I knew that being humbled had nothing to do with humiliation. God didn't want me to return to the prison of hating myself; He wanted me to exchange all of the crap, baggage, and lies for healing, freedom and an identity rooted in the power of His authority.

|FIGHTING WORDS|: *You are blessed when you get your inside world –your mind and heart-put right. Then you can see God in the outside world.* (Matthew 5:8 MSG).

Pray these words as you let go of your past and your need to control your future: "Lord, humble me."

{When We Are Who He Is}

"The meaning of our lives emerges in the surrender of ourselves to an adventure of becoming who we are not yet."

–Brennan Manning, Abbas Child

Sometimes I think we get confused about what surrender really is. To surrender is to give up all that we think we aren't. To give up the idea that we know the exact paths we are determined will lead to our dreams. To give up our need for comfort, our entitlements, our rights. To say, "What you have for me Lord is better than anything I could ever imagine or dream of." To be in a place of such raw vulnerability, that we slip Him on as our identity. To live in full confidence that we were created by Him, for Him, and that we are powered by Him so that we will do even greater works (John 14:12). To surrender means we no longer own the lies spoken over us.

In surrender there is no room for jealousy. In surrender there is no room for insecurity. To surrender means that we believe there is power in the name of Jesus to break the chains holding us in darkness or despair or worse, spiritual complacency. In surrender we embrace the amazing, unique, and beautiful parts of who we are so much so that we can't wait to live a life that showcases God's work in us!

To surrender is a form of worship; it's being made whole and being able to recognize the lies instead of getting lost in them. Surrender is a confession that God's Word really isn't too good to be true. Surrender is real and raw and messy and beautiful and redeeming and healing.

Surrender is saying, "Lord, all I need is you," and then living like we actually believe that's true. Surrender is the beginning and ending of it all. To know that my journey through past sin, failures, and fears is a story only I can tell turns the seemingly dark corners of my history into weapons that will powerfully destroy the enemy and set captives free.

STOP and take some time to write down what surrender looks like in your life.

PRAY WITH ME: Lord, today I break the lies that I am too much or not enough. Today I ask your covering over my life. Not a covering for safety, but a covering of Your grace and might and power. So that in Your Spirit I can live an outrageous life that doesn't stop at moving mountains but shakes the foundations of the whole earth. I am Yours, and I surrender...even if I have to do it 300 times today. I lift up my hands and cry out, "I surrender God! And I'm ready for more of you!"

{Not Mine to Hold}

"Let go, let go, let go." Those words looped through my head for almost a week. And not because I had just watched *Frozen*. God was asking me to believe. God was asking me to stop trying to be in control. I felt a rumbling, a shift, and an *increase* coming. As I prayed for God to increase my faith, I was faced with an opportunity to do just that. I sat at my kitchen counter that morning writing in the solemnness of the unknown. We were about to see a specialist who would test our unborn little one, not due until July of that year, for a severe heart defect and possibly Down's Syndrome.

My husband's anthem through all of our childbearing years — through the autism diagnosis of two sons, through four miscarriages and early stages of uterine cancer, through losing everything we had and being jobless had been: *WAITING IS THE HARDEST PART OF HOPE.*

That morning we waited in HOPE. Knowing that God could heal our boy, and knowing in our weakness He revels in showing His strength. Hope whispered in my ear, "This boy will be used mightily. He will have a powerful testimony before he even meets this world. People will know My grace and love and peace because of this little one!" Praise Jesus. Those words were comforting to hear, but honestly they hadn't actually breached the hard outer layers of my heart that was preparing itself for yet another heartache.

As I worshiped that morning I heard the words, "He is not yours to hold." Like Hannah, I had prayed for so long for this little man, not as long as she had for Samuel, but I know my son had been prayed into being after several miscarriages. Still, he was not mine to hold. Hannah promised Samuel to the Lord, and I knew our Charlie, a "Scrappy Warrior" along with his brothers, Sawyer "My Prayer Warrior," Thatcher a "Healer in the Making," and Crew "My Warrior Shepherd" were all God's, too. They are mine to raise but not to hold on to.

In the gut-wrenching angst of the unknown, I knew I should praise God for the chance to increase my faith but my heart wasn't really there so instead I praised God for the little men we get to teach and raise for His glory. I praised God that no label or "disability" can keep Him from transforming human weakness into a warrior spirit.

| *FIGHTING WORDS* |: *But forget all that — it is nothing compared to what I am going to do. For I am about to do something new. See, I have already begun! Do you not see it I will make a pathway through the wilderness? I will create rivers in the dry wasteland.* (Isaiah 43:18-19 NLT).

Charlie Fisher was born completely healthy on June 30th, 2013. I remember that morning I spent in anguish at my kitchen counter every day when I pick up my joyful, scrappy, healthy little boy. We experienced a healing and a powerful miracle that came with surrendering the plans we had already made for our sweet baby boy and trusting that no matter what happened God was going to move mountains with the story He was writing in our lives.

Is there something God has given you to steward (but not own) that you can't let go of? Why are you afraid to surrender it? Do you trust God? No, in your guts…do you really trust that He wants infinitely more for you than you could ever imagine? What will it take for you to let it go? How will surrendering whatever God is asking you to surrender change your life?

{Submission: It's Not Actually a Four-Letter Word}
My stomach has always twitched whenever I hear the "S" word…no not that one, the other one. Submission. (That was me whispering the word.) Why is it so hard to say? Why is it so gut-wrenchingly hard to do? I feel like it goes against my core, my human nature, my existence. Why? Because it does. Because for years that word has been used to beat women down, steal our callings, and limit our place in the Kingdom of God. A word God meant to bring freedom and fulfillment has instead been turned into a command for women to forgo their place as equal heirs to His throne.

My pastor, Ron, once said: "Our reaction to anything in life speaks more about the state of our own hearts than to what we're actually reacting to."

Before I understood this, whenever someone challenged me with the word *submit*, I put one finger up (my pointer finger people, sheesh!) with my other hand on my hip and did the ever rebellious head bob, saying: "Oh *he-e-e-elll* no." Can you see how this may have complicated my life, my marriage, and my friendships?

As I sifted out my need for control, I found it had its ugly claws lodged into so many areas in my life I couldn't break free on my own. I am so thankful to God for gently showing me these areas. Even in His gentleness, even knowing He only wants me to be free to experience Him, I was on a cyclical roller coaster of letting it go and then white knuckling again it out of fear.

If I let go of control, would I lose me? If I submitted fully to God would my voice be lost? Would I be less of a person? Would the me I thought was really "me" cease to exist? This is the craziness that consumed my thoughts.

The journey of getting married and having kids took me to places I never could have imagined: some places incredible, some not so great. A few years into the journey, I felt like parts of me were missing, like my only identity was as "his wife" or "their mom." It's like the fun, bubbly old me was traded in for an exhausted, butt wiping, puke cleaning, shell of a woman.

As I began to emerge from that stage of life, having fewer butts to wipe and less puke to clean, I found myself fighting to be the old me again. The problem was, I got confused and started picking the wrong fight. Instead of allowing the incredible things God had started in me to resurface—instead of seeking to be covered by Him and embrace the quirky, unique girl I once was, I honestly just got angry because I didn't even know where to start. I had lost myself, and while I definitely loved God, we weren't really on speaking terms. Or if we were, I just couldn't hear Him over the roaring of my need for control.

In his book *Why Not Women*, Loren Cunningham says, "Submission to God is the ultimate strength." He goes on to say, "True freedom comes when we submit to one another in humility."

What does freedom in relationship even look like? Are you someone who needs to be in control? Think about it carefully. For years I told myself I was an easy going, "go with the flow" type of person until one day I realized I was only that way when things went exactly how I planned. (That's control in case you were wondering.) We are called to submit to one another because it mirrors the relationship of the

Trinity. There's a beautiful harmony to it, it's what makes relationships work, both with people and with God. It's in understanding the importance and meaning of submission that I finally understood the idea of dying to myself and becoming less ("less" as in less of the parts of me He never intended me to be) so that He could become more.

|*FIGHTING WORDS*|: *Sitting down, He called the twelve and said to them, "If anyone wants to be first, he shall be last of all and servant of all"* (Mark 9:35 NIV).

{Shake it up, Baby}
Surrender may sound heavy and hard. It's like reading directions and getting to one of those steps where you ask yourself, "Do I really need to do this part? It's probably faster to skip it." Maybe that's just me because I hate reading directions. But here's the thang with surrender and letting go; if we try to skip over it and pretend like it doesn't exist, we'll miss out on parts of God we never even knew about. I think of surrender as a picture of a body entangled with thick vines representing all the things we were never meant to be and all that we were never meant carry. Those things entangle us, growing their roots way down deep until we're completely covered and we can't even see the real us anymore.

When we surrender to God, we're giving Him permission to strip off the vines, to pull out those painful, poisonous roots. When we allow Him to heal our pasts, we can take steps forward again. When we can accept His love and forgiveness, we can then extend it to others who have hurt us. When we can embrace the beauty in our existence, we can let go of every lie that tells us we're not enough. If we give God permission to strip away the vines and rip their roots out of deep painful places, He will. He will weed our gardens and heal us by filling those wounds and gashes and deep wells of hurt with the soothing salve of His Spirit. Our willingness to surrender actually sets us free.

Some of us who have experienced a lot of pain and rejection try to hold on to those roots because even though they are lies, at least they are lies that mask and protect us deep down where it really hurts. They keep us from fully feeling, they keep us from having to engage on a level that could wound us even more than a little root being ripped out. So we keep those vines that protect and hide who we really are. We learn the language and play the part. We may say "yes" to God, but it's a surface "yes." We know He's there, but we don't let Him get close and go deep. Our experience of Him is filtered through the thick layers of vines that bind us. Our "yes" to God has little to do with intimacy or living in His power and everything to do with keeping up appearances. Our yes becomes a performance and honestly it's exhausting.

I was in my mid thirties before I realized I was living

in bondage. As in the majority of my life was lived behind the bars my fears had built. And even after I knew it seemed easier to live a slave to my fear and insecurity than to have my guts ripped out by the process of surrender. I was sure all of me would be left too weak, too vulnerable, and too exposed to recover, and I wasn't sure I really wanted what God had for me *that* badly.

Sounds thrilling right? Just what everyone dreams of to end a long day: sit down, read a book, and oh yeah, have your guts ripped out. But the beauty of surrender is that your guts aren't actually ripped out. While parts might be painful, it's actually quite beautiful, empowering, and it always ends in freedom.

In Luke 11:13 (NLT) it says, "If you sinful people know how to give good gifts to your children, how much more will your heavenly Father give the Holy Spirit to those who ask him?"

You've gotta deal with your stuff. You just have to or you'll be wandering around your entire life blaming others for why you aren't living the life you were created to live. He wants to heal you and set you free. He wants you to live a life of adventure and abundance, but you can't do that if you're carrying around years of baggage. You can't be free if you've chosen to give bitterness, un-forgiveness, and anger permanent residence in your life. This is the part where I want you to imagine me and hordes of other women cheering you on! This is the part where I want you to press in and hear God whispering: "You're worth it, let go of all of that other stuff!" This is the part where you get to choose to be a slave to your past or take your rightful place as an heir to the King. Freedom or slavery? Bondage or healing? Only you can make the choice. What's it going to be?

PRAY WITH ME: Lord today I choose to be FREE. Break me out of this bondage. Remove the heavy vines of bitterness, anger, fear, insecurity and unforgiveness. Thank you, Lord. Forgive me Jesus for holding on; forgive my rebellion and pride ultimately rooted in the fear of being unimportant, unloved, and unvalued. I know this couldn't be further from your heart. Forgive me for seeking an identity apart from you. Remind me that it's in surrender that my true creative, beautifully unique self can soar. Restore me Jesus… thank you for tenderly opening my eyes to this barrier between us! I receive Your freedom, I am Yours. I SURRENDER… I lift up my hands and cry out, "I surrender, God! And I'm ready for MORE of You!"

This is a great spot to take a break. Close the book and process what you just read. If you run past it because it feels scary or overwhelming, you're going to miss out on so much! Just press the pause button, turn on some music, or sit in silence and have a quiet conversation with the Artist who formed you by hand. Ask Him to make clear what needs to be surrendered in your life. Then ask Him what He wants to exchange all of your burdens for... I guarantee the answer will involve *more* of Him in some capacity.

FOUR: TRUE GRIT

What is grit? GRIT is waking up in the morning wondering how you will encounter God today.

GRIT is looking in the mirror and seeing the beauty of God's creation instead of the baggage of years passed.

GRIT is knowing who and whose you are so you can be confident enough to call others into their destinies.

GRIT is unleashing heaven on earth even when your feelings don't match what you know to be true.

GRIT is loving so outrageously it makes people hunger for God.

GRIT is living in freedom when the world whispers lies of bondage in your ear.

GRIT heals the broken hearted and isn't afraid to set the prisoners free.

GRIT celebrates beauty in ashes and embraces the awkward in life.

GRIT is the decision to turn failure, abuse, abandonment, or heartache into a story of powerful victory.

GRIT doesn't need praise to keep serving and moving forward.

GRIT surrenders with humility to love when the world says "you deserve…"

GRIT is celebrating someone else's success even when you feel discouraged in your own dreams.

GRIT is knowing you have influence.

GRIT is boldly living in the overflow of the Holy Spirit.

GRIT is knowing when it's time to say yes and having the gumption to strike the ax.

GRIT is warring for someone with no agenda or expectation of returned love.

GRIT dreams unreasonable dreams and then looks for God given opportunity to dare the impossible.

Hungry for more? Thirsty for something truly

quenching? Empty in places you can't describe? Well then, we've got to stop chasing perfection and passionately pursue God's love.

When we live this, feel this, yearn for this... We are living with GRIT, AND GRIT IS SO GOOD!

Three things determine how fearless we are... who we say we are, how we love others and how we've encountered God. These three things shape and shade how we move forward with what God has given us. Three things have the power to change everything we thought we knew about ourselves and the powerful story God has written for our lives.

|FIGHTING WORDS|: Then I heard the Lord asking, "Whom should I send as a messenger to this people? Who will go for us?" I said, "Here I am. Send me" (Isaiah 6:8 NLT).

Having a gritty faith is all about leaving behind what we think we deserve and what we think we're entitled to and grabbing onto something deeper, more authentic, and life-altering. Are you hungry for something more? Are you ready to get a little uncomfortable? Are you ready to get real with God? Say it with me: "YESSSSSS!"

GO: Read Numbers 14. Yep, all of it. Shoo, shoo! Go now and meet me back here when you're done.

We have to be OK with being inconvenienced, we need to stop asking others to hold our hands if we want a fresh experience with our Creator.

You have to want it. You have to be hungry. If you're not it's OK, but ask for it because a mountain-moving life can only come when we're hungry for more and fed up with ordinary.

{Leading Ladies}
I love the movie The Holiday. In it, Eli Wallach plays a witty, wise character: an old-time movie producer who worked with all of the "greats" back in the day. He describes some of the leading ladies he directed in the 40's and 50's as having gumption. While helping Kate Winslet's character find herself again after getting her heart broken, he tells her: "Iris, in the movies we have leading ladies, and we have the best friend. You, I can tell, are a leading lady, but for some reason you are behaving like the best friend." To which she responds, "You're so right. You're supposed to be the leading lady of your own life, for God's sake!"

So here's the question… Are you the leading lady of your own life for God's sake? No, I really mean for His sake? Or are you the best friend, always cheering on others, always the shoulder to cry on, but never having enough gumption or GRIT to step up and say: "Here I am, Lord, use me!"?

{Mountains}

Mountains start to move when we decide that just playing the part isn't enough. Mountains shake when we hunger for more of Him. In our intimacy with Him, the foundation of our lives begins to tremble... and the mountains of our lives awaken and MOVE.

It's in this intimacy — this sacred place with God — that we start to shift from the safety of the known and the convenient. More Lord, more, more...We cry out but don't believe our own words. We say words that sound like love, but then we choose to live in offense because the love we know is flawed and full of our own agenda. So our mountains stand firm and we question God and His promises.

We long for significance, and when the praise of men is no longer satisfying we question: "Does God really have for me what He claims"?

YES! A thousand times, Yes! But it only comes through a life full of Him.

In the poverty of uniqueness, we're determined to look like those we adore. But in drowning ourselves in the Spirit, we emerge, stunning, new, and significant. Bold, courageous, creative, artistic...we now hunger for the only true thing that makes us matter.

We long for the spectacular, for scandalous redemption, for mind-blowing restoration. And then He comes stirring hearts, opening minds, and healing pasts.

You have been saved for purpose: for greatness. To be a life-giver and to love so radically people have no choice but to be healed by experiencing Christ's Spirit *in you*. God has rescued YOU. You could be in any stage of your journey with Him as you read these words, but what I want you to see today is being rescued is just the beginning of the journey. Being rescued is the event that marks the jumping off place where you will either tell God: "I believe what you have for me. I trust you, and I'm willing to endure whatever I have to in order to fully know you." OR you will see the giants ahead of you and turn back; longing for the bondage of your old life like the Israelites did (remember Numbers 14).

Joshua and Caleb had seen and experienced the abundance of what God was trying to give the entire nation of Israel. They were the only two who could see past the giants and trust that God would deliver on His promise. Here's something you have to know. When you make the choice to *go*, when you decide to trust God over worldly wisdom or even the advice of people closest to you, it will scare people. Did you love the part in Numbers 14:10 where the whole community wanted to stone Joshua and Caleb? (By love I meant: did you almost wet your pants and say,

"What the crap?") Maybe that's just me. It wasn't enough that those boys were trusting God to fight the giants; they also had to stand up and be bold and courageous in what had to have felt like gut-wrenching betrayal by their own community. The people they loved and did life with wanted to KILL them for saying YES to God and trusting what He said was true.

When we say "yes," we're saying "yes" to it all. That's why it takes GRIT to move forward. It's not for the faint of heart. But good news: He designed you, YOU to be uniquely qualified to withstand the hardships and challenges that come with a life of substance, so you can then move forward to conquer the giants in your life.

"Wow," you say. "Sounds fun. Excuse me while I go update my Facebook status or read something that won't give me nightmares." Don't go...because I promise you, the freedom and love and life you will receive from continuing to move forward far exceeds any giant you may face along the way.

If it was easy, everyone would be doing it. If Jesus' message was a flowery, feel-good, cuddly hug, then puking smiley faces across our social media feeds and saying God bless you would feel like enough. But it's more than that. His story is one of redemption through surrender—a love so deep and raw and real that He withstood betrayal and murder so we could know Him and live freely through Him. Maybe a life of ease with a checklist faith sounds good to you, but it breeds emptiness, and you will miss out because you'll have no God given gumption, no testimony of God's greatness, no compassion-building pain. Life would feel fake and surface level, and whether you know it or not, at some point you will want more.

How can we cry out to God and beg Him to show us His will for our lives and who He designed us to be and then balk at walking forward when it seems scary or overwhelming? God wants us to move past the fear of the awkward and unknown and to really believe He can do what He says He will.

{Who do You Think You Are?}
"When God tells you who you are, who you are not has to go." -Bob Hazlett, Roar

It seems like every time I make a move toward God, either literally or spiritually, there's a burst of excitement followed by a whisper; "Who do you think you are?" This question always brings on thoughts, fears, and whispers of my doubts about who God made me to be.

I look at others, who are so intimate with God, and I long for a closeness to Him that overflows into the rest of my life, my community, and my world, but sometimes I'm afraid. And I hear the whispers again:

"What if He doesn't have that kind of relationship for you? What if you're nothing special? Who do you think you are?"

Jealousy is an ugly thing. Wanting what somebody else has only keeps us from having what's right in front of us. And what is right in front of all of us is something fresh and exciting and adventurous. It's a work He has already begun.

I had a full on melt down one Monday night at Fight Night. As I mentioned earlier, Fight Night is a local gathering of women in a room above a bar — an amazing time of worship and healing. On this particular Fight Night, we heard an awesome message about love — the real kind, full of bravery and grit. Then we challenged a room full of women to open up about what keeps them from loving others. As women talked and wept and prayed and healed, three of us stood up front and prayed over the room.

I had come that night dry, weary, tired, and feeling a little jealous, if I'm being honest, of a few friends who seem to have the most AMAZING connection to our Creator. I had arrived with the familiar feeling that I was always on the edge but unable to jump. I had simply entered into the routine of Fight Night: set up, greet people, be funny, pray, and then pass the mic to someone God is speaking through mightily. As I prepared to wrap up a great night, one of the women

I was praying with up front directed the prayer toward me…and I broke. As she spoke these words I wept: "Lindsay, He is hovering over you with such joy, waiting for you to come to Him. He's waiting for you Lindsay with such joy."

Earlier that week, I had a dream: while streaking from my bedroom to my laundry room to grab my undies (in all of my "natural glory"), everyone from the Extreme Makeover build was looking through my windows. I couldn't hide, and I was so embarrassed. When I woke up, I wondered if it meant I was going to be exposed. Apparently it did. At least I was able to enjoy the rawness of my meltdown fully clothed this time! It was in the rawness and truth of the words my friend spoke over me that I had to confess my jealousy and receive God's word that HE was waiting for me. That instead of trying to recreate the faith I saw my friends having, He was waiting to overflow me with His Spirit, and it's only through that overflow that His powerful, mountain-moving gifts could flourish in me.

{Falling off a Truck: Grit, Gumption, and Victory}
"Victory is a gift. Empty your hands and take the gift."
                                                        –E. Stanley Jones

In 2012 my family and I decided to empty our hands and take the gift. Loving all things old, rusty, and vintage-y, we decided to use the property God had given us the year before to host a vintage fair. We invited vintage, antique, furniture, and junk dealers from around the West Coast to come and sell.

We booked great local bands, food, and wine and we were gunna party! Our problem: our very "rustic" farm was in the process of being "revitalized" (that's putting it nicely). Years of neglect had created an ambiance more suited to a scrap yard than a high-end, boutique shopping experience.

We spent the summer mucking out a barn filled with a 100 years of trash in 100-degree heat. Our days were filled with cuts, scrapes, bruises, sweat, tears, and grumpy, tired kids whining to go home. In the thick of it, I didn't see the victory; I saw dirt and smelled like B.O. But when it was finished, we took a picture of our work that still makes my heart leap. One of the treasures this farm came with is a rusty old flatbed Ford farm truck. Her tires are flat and, she doesn't run, but man is she purdy. The night we finished, we snapped a picture of my mom and I jumping for joy off the back of the truck bed to celebrate our work. Little did I know, there was more muck to follow, but still, that picture symbolizes the victory of moving forward, and that's something to celebrate!

We had no clue we'd have the outpouring of people who wanted to come and see what a vintage fair even was. In the first hour of the first day of the fair, I got in a hurry, tried to hurdle a mini fence (we're talking 18 inches high), and broke my ankle. But even with that little hiccup, the fair ended up being amazing. We had incredible talent take residence on our beat-up little farm. With only Facebook in our marketing toolbox, we were able to pull in about 1,800 shoppers. More importantly, God showed us that even when things feel mind-boggling impossible, He is there to give us victory.

Funny enough, we almost didn't go through with the vintage fair. Even though it's now a growing annual event that our valley looks forward to, we almost didn't have the guts to pull the trigger. It took us months to get up the nerve to even put the idea out there to our friends and family. Panic attacks, with fear, and insecurity almost kept us from moving forward. As excited as we were to bring something new and unique to our town, whispers of doubt clouded our faith for what God was trying to accomplish. *"Who do you think you are? What do you think you're doing? This is going to fail. What if it rains? What if no one comes? Why would you even try?"* These were just some of the whispers we heard.

On a side note, when you KNOW God is asking you to do something and you hear whispers like those, it's pretty much a green light to go, and it's a huge indicator that the enemy doesn't want you to move.

Here's the beautiful thing about victory: it is sweeter, deeper, and even more mind-blowing than we can imagine when it's the result of putting yourself out there—stepping out of your comfort zone and into God's "yes."

Sometimes we get so focused on labeling the goal or outcome of a certain event or season of life as "victory" that we don't see the real victory; the character-building, and the Spirit-filling God-experience that's in the depth of whatever it is we are trying to conquer. It is in the journey, the trenches, and the front line battles filled with blood, sweat and sometimes B.O. that He gives us the gift of victory. It is when we are beaten down and surrender all that we are because we know we can't take one more step on our own, that He steps in—our victory nailed to His hands and feet. And when we look back, we probably wondered why we tried to do it on our own in the first place.

{From Funk to Freedom}

|*FIGHTING WORDS*|: *"Today when you hear his voice, don't harden your hearts as Israel did when they rebelled, when they tested me in the wilderness."* (Hebrews 3:8 NLT).

"Where the spirit of the Lord is there is freedom" (2 Corinthians 3:17 NIV) is one of my favorite verses EVER. But what about where the Spirit of the Lord is *not*? Where the Spirit of the Lord is *not* there is legalism, there is burn out, and there is an abundance of critical and hardened hearts. The thing is, we can be speaking the same words and living the same life (on the outside) but what's on the inside can be something very different and anything but life giving.

A while ago I was crying out to God, wondering why I was so dry and empty on the inside. If I'm honest, even my cries had been half-hearted. Sometimes, I do to God what my kids do to me. Like when one of my boys sits on the couch yelling at me to get him a drink of water. When I tell him to get it himself, the level of drama increases, and I hear things like, "I can't take it anymore, I'm dying of thirst!" Or: "But my legs hurt, and I can't walk to the kitchen." If anyone else was listening, they would probably jump up and get the little drama king whatever he wanted. But as the mom, I know he's capable of getting up. I know he just wants me to do for him what he's too lazy to do for himself. So I say, "Well…I guess you're not *that* thirsty then." Eventually he miraculously gets up and gets a drink or forgets he was thirsty in the first place and goes on playing or watching TV.

What's the point? We want the revival experience. We want to live in the power of Christ. We want all that He has for us, but sometimes we want all of it without actually doing anything about it. We "cry out" in prayer, and He answers us saying, "I'm right here, I never left. Stop asking others to do for you what you need to do yourself. What you need is right in front of you, I've already provided it…all you have to do is get your butt off the couch and go get it." He has everything waiting for us. All we have to do is move forward. Through the awkward, through the sometimes painful and scary, we have to stand up and make the decision to forgive and love and to take steps toward Him, even when we're afraid.

I spent a two-month season of my life completely pouting. I was angry and hurt and discouraged and unwilling to get up and move toward what God had promised me. The problem was the funk grew so gradually; I didn't even realize what was happening. It set in like a subtle sickness and then spread like a cancer. What started as a dark seed of selfishness and passivity, bloomed into something dull and dry and ordinary. AWESOME. I finally woke up and realized *I* was the one who had stopped talking to God, who had stopped reading His words, who had distanced myself from Him because He hadn't done what I wanted Him to do in the time frame I wanted him to do it in.

We can't spread life and revival without being filled with HIS LIFE and HIS REVIVAL. There are no words or works that can ever replace the POWER and MIGHT that mark the life of a person filled with the Holy Spirit. We can try to duplicate it, but all attempts will come up empty and feel like old religion. It's easier to play a part than to actually be filled with Him. It's easier to control a situation than to risk being broken. It's easier to whine about what we think we deserve than to surrender what we think we need. But *how* we know Him is how we share Him and expose others to Him.

We have to stop trying to imitate and recreate what only HE can do. We are His unique creation. He is ready to do something new, in fact he has already started... we just have to be willing to let go and believe that what He has for us is eons more extravagant than anything we could ever try to do ourselves.

{"Goffing It"}

I have a friend named Jenna who makes me do things I don't want to do. Things that make me pitty (that's actually her term). She is my fearless ambassador, and I love her so very much! We first 'met' when she sent me an email out of the blue one day. I didn't know her but we had mutual friends, and she asked me to come speak to her college group. I said yes. Little did I know it was one of the very first steps into my journey of saying yes to God. To thank me for speaking, she gave me a brand new book by a guy name Bob Goff, called: *Love Does*. Even though I had no clue who he was or what the book was about, I actually knew it was going to be a life changer.

I wasn't wrong. Once I picked the booked up, God used this man's words to change me at my core. His message was simple: love people and say yes to God, no matter what. It was about being defined by Christ's love and letting everything else go. One of the things Bob Goff said that punched me in the gut was: "He's asking: will you take what you think defines you, leave it behind and let me define who you are instead?" (*Love Does*, 92).

Homina! Allowing Him to define who we are while we surrender everything else is one of the biggest weapons we can have in our arsenal. Bob's a lover, and I'm a fighter, but our goal is the same: to let the love and grace of Jesus push us through even when we're afraid to move forward.

From that book forth, Jenna and I call diving into really big, scary, squidgy things "Goffing It." A few months ago, I got a call to be the main speaker at a women's retreat for one of the biggest churches in our valley. I said yes. Knowing God has given me everything I need, I was excited to meet with the women's ministry leaders. By excited I actually mean terrified out of my mind and close to wetting my pants because I was sure they'd asked the wrong person. I asked Jenna if she thought I was going to be too much for these women. I tend to feel like I need to reel it in a lot because…well… sometimes I'm a lot to take in. I have a hard time filtering thoughts and almost always give my opinion whether you want it or not. She assured me I was about to meet with some awesome women who could handle my brand of crazy.

Sometimes it's just saying yes to an email from a friend. Sometimes it's yes to leaving behind any shame, guilt or regrets from the past bogging us down. Sometimes it's saying yes even when we're not sure what we're saying yes to, but we know it's where God is leading us. *"Goffing It"* looks different for everyone, but big or small; all you have to do is say yes with your life.

||Public Service Announcement: This YES business I'm talking about is SAYING YES TO GOD. This is not saying yes to friends who don't know boundaries and organizations that know you won't say no. It's important to know the difference. End of PSA.||

Here's the bottom line: saying yes to God doesn't ensure success in the eyes of society. Saying yes to God ensures a fuller realization of who He is and hopefully more opportunities to encounter Him on deeper levels. The truth is, saying yes is risky and can be so incredibly awkward at times you'll want to crawl back into the womb. But Jenna has also taught me that it's in the awkward that we grow and develop character. It's in the awkward that relationships are cemented and friendships turn into sisterhood. While it's human nature to walk around awkward, Jenna has challenged me to dive into it head first, and there's nothing grittier than that.

|*FIGHTING WORDS*|: *Don't copy the behavior and customs of this world, but let God transform you into a new person by changing the way you think. Then you will learn to know God's will for you, which is good and pleasing and perfect."* (Romans 12:2 NLT).

Have you been trying to avoid awkward in your life? Is it time to say yes to something that scares you, knowing it's a risk? It's your turn to *"Goff It."* It's your turn to dare and dream and get a little pitty. Are you ready? It's time. Normal is boring. Let's dive into awkward together!

SIDE NOTE: If you want to dive deeper into the concept of embracing awkward you *must* check out Jenna's book *Awkward: A 30-Day Challenge.* IT WILL ROCK YOU! *(Visit www.jennabenton.com)*

What has been holding you back from taking the first steps forward? Here are some common answers:
I don't know what He wants me to move forward in.
I am afraid of what people will think.
I am under-qualified, and every time I think of moving forward I hear the words, "Who do you think you are?" Or, "What makes you think you're so special?"
It's safer to do what I know.
What will happen if...?
I have responsibilities, I can't just...

What if I'm wrong? How do I know?

Do you ever try to recreate things yourself that really God should be doing? Pssssst... Be honest with yourself because you're not alone. I've done it A LOT. I want the relationship and abundance of the Holy Spirit I see in others, but sometimes I am too impatient, prideful, controlling or afraid to fully trust that if I let go, God will actually blow my mind within His presence.

Do you ever want what others have? Not stuff really...I'm talking influence, ministry, gifts, relationships or abilities?

Do you believe that God wants to use you to move mountains in his kingdom? Or do you believe that he only uses "other" people to do that kind of work?

I once listened to a Circuit Rider podcast that was filled with African prayers of revival. In it Brian Brennt led his students through the most powerful prayers I have ever heard. Today we're going to borrow parts of these life-giving, revival-laden appeals to conjure up some breakthrough in our own lives. Here's my paraphrase of those prayers:

PRAY WITH ME: *Jesus, I want you more than anything. I want to live a life bursting with faith that is not bound by fear. Lift the scales from my eyes! Remind me that I am worthy of the life you've called me to because YOU*

MADE ME. In your name, I ask you to bind the enemy and BREAK the lies he's held over my life! I speak to every yoke working against spiritual growth in my life to BREAK in the name of Jesus! Every destructive habit designed to waste my calling, DIE in the name of Jesus! Lord fill me with your life-giving Spirit so I can go out and share you with others. I receive your fresh anointing in the name of Jesus.

FIVE: WONDER

{Adventure is Calling}

For my 35th birthday, my husband gave me the gift of my dreams. A weekend ALONE. Is that bad? Apparently not everyone fantasizes about being alone in the wilderness, but alone is how I recharge. It's one of my love languages. Alone is how I encounter God's wonder in the most intimate way. Alone is my sacred place and I crave it. All of the other hermits out there are saying amen to this.

Never having this opportunity before my husband's gift, I took the utmost care in planning my 48 hours of peace. I wanted a cabin in the woods, off the beaten path, but still within cell range. I'm the stereotypical Oregonian in a lot of ways, and I love the outdoors. I experience God in such a deeper way in the stillness and peace of His creation and I knew this weekend was going to be life altering.

I found a cute little craftsman bungalow on Klamath Lake. The lake is beautiful to look at but apparently filled with leaches and algae, so swimming was swiftly taken off of the agenda.

I pulled up to a gorgeous but very empty lodge. It felt a little eerie as I let myself in to cabin #1, and the first thought that entered my mind was, "I wonder if anyone has ever been murdered here?" Every scene from every scary movie I've ever watched flashed before my eyes, and I may have peed a little.

I met the people in the cabin next to me. They were nice, a little too nice. I thought about taking pictures of their truck and license plate because I was sure they were ax murderers waiting for their next victim. I texted C.J. and said maybe I should just come home or maybe he should throw our four boys in the truck and come visit. I could almost feel his eyes rolling as I read his text. "You're fine, don't come home." I'm so glad I listened to him. Apparently the ominous feeling my "too nice" neighbors gave me was the outpouring of too many network TV crime dramas and not actually a prophetic revelation. My weekend was filled with writing, exploring, and hiking. I worshiped and prayed and just soaked in His presence. It was perfect.

Whenever I'm out in the wilderness, Psalm 46 rushes my mind. Be still and know that I am God. We like to pop that verse out of the chapter and it sounds nice...it sounds like an excuse to do nothing. But it's in the midst of God displaying his mightiness that He asks us to be still and KNOW He is God. More than asking us to physically be still, He's asking us to take in all that He is and to let Him be our refuge and strength...to be our source of courage and to just be in awe of His power. To be still is to stop striving and trying to do ourselves what He has already done within us.

My trip was full of wonder and God's voice because I was able to slow down and take time to fully experience Him. From the act of slowing down and intentionally worshipping, a natural outpouring of adventure found its way into the weekend. For me, wonder is just the realization that all God says He is, is actually true. It's the acceptance of His promises, and it's the saturation of His hope and presence. You don't have to be alone in the woods for this to happen, of course. When we say yes to God, when we experience His wonder, when we slip into our sacred place, we feel like we can do anything. Wonder is the birthplace of adventure and the launching pad for a life that is anything but ordinary!

|FIGHTING WORDS|: And God raised the Lord and will also raise us up by his power (1 Corinthians 6:14 ESV)

{Wonder Boys}

I'm not sure when it happened, but somehow in the mix of snotty noses, broken bones, homeschooling, and little boy adventures; C.J. and I started to refer to our crazy clan as our *"wonder boys."* Partially, I think because their little minds are always full of wonder and adventure and partly because of the amazing way they live out those adventures. We have a lover, an artist, a flying squirrel, and our little "Charzilla". They all amaze me. The way these kids love and experience life is more than inspiring. I think everyone on the planet is hungering for the same thing: WONDER.

We want to know what our purpose is and what our gifts are. We want to be fed and inspired. We want to make a difference and have influence. So we read the newest trendy self-help books, we start the coolest new church programs, we put in to practice all of the things "good" people do in life...but still we come up short. When we lay our head down on the pillow at night there's a certain emptiness, a loneliness, a longing for more. So we wake up the next morning and pray: "Lord help me accomplish all of the things I need to accomplish today to make a difference." Because we need to invite God to be a part of our journey, right? We need God to help us execute the plans we've put in place. We need God to help us through that 10-step program to whatever new happiness is just beyond our grasp. And before we know it, something has happened. We've replaced glory, majesty and wonder with our own ability to get things done.

When we do all of the "things" we think we're supposed to and we still come up short of the wonder and power and adventure God has for us, I think it's clear that we need to step back and ask ourselves why it's *not* working.

Do you know what God created us for? It wasn't so we'd invite Him to join us in life. He created us to love Him, to partner with Him, and to love others with Him.

Is it time to be still and welcome the Holy Spirit back to the helm of your life?

|FIGHTING WORDS|: "God will do this, for he is faithful to do what he says, and he has invited you into partnership with his Son, Jesus Christ our Lord."
(1 Corinthians 1:9 NLT).

Sometimes I think we get confused. We tuck God neatly into the little compartmentalized box we allow Him to have dominion over in our lives. We decide what loving and experiencing God looks like, and we're content to just go to church on Sunday, maybe have a daily a 15-minute quiet time, and of course paste a Christian bumper sticker on our car.

I'm not mocking or pointing fingers. Instead of a bumper sticker I have the ichthus tattooed on my back. I've lived this journey. I've been bound by a definition of love that leaves me empty and unsatisfied. I've been weighed down by the chains of religion and routine and the sting of never quite being able to experience God in a way that changes everything. Wonder is birthed when we refuse that kind of life and simply ask God for more of Him.

{The Wonder of Love}
What does it look like to love Him? Well what does it look like to love your spouse or child or your best friend? Love looks like time spent together, having fun together, weathering tragedy together, going deep together. Love for God looks like actually loving other people, through wounds and without judgment. Love looks like just *being* sometimes, and through that *just being with Him*, comes the increase of our ability to accept His love and grace over us.

We have to stop striving for what we want and just be IN LOVE with Him. His love language is LOVE. His expectation is LOVE. His gift to us is LOVE in the form of favor, power, authority, and grace.

So, if you're feeling a little withered and dry inside, if you're feeling the need to be revitalized, if you're feeling the need to revitalize the community around you, here's your one step program. Your one-bullet-point sermon, your one trendy plan in two words: JUST LOVE. Talk to Him like you'd talk to a good friend. Listen like you would listen to a good friend. Worship Him with gratefulness. Spend time just *being* with Him and see what happens.

For years I longed for His wonder in my life (even the years I was in full time ministry and a pastor's wife), but I have to admit I didn't really even know Him. Instead of having something sacred and intimate, I followed God like I follow a blogger I love on Instagram or Facebook. I would in essence "read His posts" and "like His pictures" and even comment from time to time. But the personal, real, wonder-building relationship with a God I can't control wasn't there.

{Open the Eyes of My Heart}
One dark September night, outside a warehouse in Central Point, Oregon, I witnessed a helicopter chase that will forever be etched in my mind. As I stood there, holding the hands of the man I loved, dressed in white, gathered with friends and family the spotlight of a helicopter shined down on the outdoor stage of our church's amphitheater. To this day people, still think our valley's only helicopter

chase was a part of our wedding ceremony. It was memorable, to say the least. As we exchanged our vows, the very loud, very bright chopper must have had a hard time differentiating a young bride from the criminal they were searching for because it circled the church for what seemed like an eternity.

Minutes before the dramatic visit from above, we had been worshipping to one of my favorite songs, "Open the Eyes of My Heart, Lord." The ceremony was magical: no frills or even very many flowers. It was just us and 480 of our closest friends and family singing in a tiki-torch-lit plot of grass. It's funny that it has taken me over 14 years to really understand the enormity of that song title. Jesus came to heal the sick, set the captives free, and make the blind see. While He did heal the blind literally, I think we often miss out on the fact that He came to open our spiritual eyes, too.

Sometimes we miss His wonder because we are spiritually blind to what's going on around us.

|FIGHTING WORDS|: Then Jesus told him, "I entered this world to render judgment – to give sight to the blind and to show those who think they can see that they are blind" (John 9:39 NLT).

A while ago, C.J. and I were reading an article 24-year-old Alistair Farland wrote before he died in the middle of a yearlong motorcycle trip from Alaska to South America. At first when C.J. started talking about it I was like: "No babe...I don't do sad for sad sake." But then he explained that the article celebrated the fact that this guy lived more in his 24 years than most people ever do. As the editor introduced Alistair's last piece of work, he wrote these words: "The things that we cannot plan are the things that define our character." (Huckberry.com, *Attitude is Everything*).

Sometimes we hold so tightly to our plans that we scarcely give the Holy Spirit room to live and breathe in our lives. Sometimes we're so focused on what we think we need that we can't see that God is offering us what He knows we can't truly live without. Is this you? Have you been white knuckling a plan because it gives you purpose, comfort, safety, or value? What does God have to say about that? Have you asked Him lately? He has so much more for us all...and so many times that MORE takes the shape of something that's not even on our radar.

Pray with me: Lord mess up our days. Mess up our schedules. Crumple our checklists. Open our eyes to how You're moving around us and help us to just delight in Your presence.

|FIGHTING WORDS|: This is what the Sovereign Lord, the Holy One of Israel, says: "Only in returning

to me and resting in me will you be saved. In quietness and confidence is your strength. But you would have none of it. (Isaiah 30:15 NLT).

CLOSE THIS BOOK. Yep, put it down. And take some time to JUST BE with God. Go outside or turn on some music. Anything that will help you turn off the craziness in your head and just engage with the Holy Spirit.

{Hunger Pangs}

I'm not a scrawny gal; I'm what my Uncle Ted calls "stout." *(Thanks for that, Uncle Ted.)* Since overcoming a major eating disorder when I was 20, I haven't been one to miss a meal, or snack, or quad venti mocha with whip. I've yoyo dieted for the past 30 years, but even on the strictest of diets, I don't know if I've really ever known hunger.

One time though, when I was 19, I went on a two-week back packing trip in the foothills of the Andes. On that camping trip, I probably came the closest to knowing what real hunger feels like as I ever will. I was fresh off the plane in Santiago, Chile to work for Iberro Americana Ministries. I only knew a few words of Spanish; I was a gringa who didn't even know what gringa meant. Needless to say, I was lost and spent the better part of six months only understanding small parts of every conversation. So, it was no surprise that I was disastrously unprepared, and under packed as

I embarked on a youth group adventure for weeks in the wilderness of southern Chile. After a two-day journey by bus, train and on foot to reach our camping spot, I found out we were supposed to bring a) snacks to last two weeks or b) money to buy snacks from the indigenous family hosting our trek.

I grew up going on camping trips arranged by my super mother, aka Betty Crocker, aka June Cleaver who packed Costco packs of chips and licorice, homemade cookies, and all the soda we could drink. We never went hungry while "roughing it" in our heavily wooded parking lot, but this was a camping trip like nothing I'd ever experienced. By the end of the two weeks, I was so hungry I was sneaking the potato peels from the garbage pile and even ate the coagulated sheep's blood no one thought I would touch with a ten foot pole. I was HUNGRY. I didn't care what it was, if it even remotely resembled food I was on it.

As I thought back on the hunger I felt on this trip, I realized that I hadn't actually felt a true hunger for God until a few years ago. Someone asked me recently what hungering for God even means and how to get it. I didn't have the answer. I don't think there's a 10-step program for it. I searched blogs and books, and while there were some decent articles, I still didn't feel like I had a grasp on how to explain it let alone get it. And I realized it's not something anyone can give to you. You can't be spoon-fed hunger. It's the yearning to know God more: not just in our dark hours, not just in the times we need Him or when we're in crisis. Hunger wants to be with Him and filled by Him when we have nothing to gain but relationship. It's longing to be in His presence, just because.

| FIGHTING WORDS |: So Jesus explained, "I tell you the truth, the Son can do nothing by himself. He does only what he sees the Father doing. Whatever the Father does, the Son also does. For the Father loves the Son and shows him everything he is doing. In fact, the Father will show him how to do even greater works than healing this man. Then you will truly be astonished. For just as the Father gives life to those he raises from the dead, so the Son gives life to anyone he wants."
(John 5:19-21 NLT).

I struggle with this. I have an agenda for almost everything. I get things done, and if at all possible, I like to kill two birds with one stone. Who has time to sit around in a secret quiet place and in the stillness know that He is there? It's hard to type these words, they actually make my heart ache a bit — real confessions often do.

I was talking to a friend about how to become hungry. We both agreed that it might be as simple as recognizing that we want to want more of God in our lives, even if we don't know exactly what that "more" looks like.

God wants us to want Him, to need Him, and to love Him...even when we're doing fine. Even when life is OK, or good, or even great. *That's hunger.*

I want God to overshadow, overpower, and overflow in my life. Does that always happen? No, because my own insecurities and fear can royally wreck things sometimes. But I want it, and He knows I want it, and I think that's enough.

It doesn't matter how we feel. God isn't more God when we feel excited and on fire for Him, and He isn't less God when we're moody, down or PMS-y. He is the constant; He is not the feeling. Even when we're too exhausted, scared, intimidated, or discouraged to want more of Him, we can call out the things that are not yet as if they are and tell Him that we want to want Him more.

| FIGHTING WORDS | : "(as it is written, 'I have made you a father of many nations') in the presence of Him whom believed-God, who gives life to the dead and call those things which do not exist as though they did." (Romans 4:17 ESV).

{Wonder Bread}
You know how when you eat really processed junk food, you feel full for a little bit but then find

yourself hungry for more soon after? You're really just craving more of the empty calories though, not the good stuff.

Being satisfied with surface-level christianese religion is like the empty calories; it's a great way to fake us into thinking we're spiritually full, when really we're just full of crap. Always being the one in crisis, always making everything about us and how we feel, always measuring our yes by how comfortable we'll be, always having canned answers to complicated problems...these things clog us up. You can't be spiritually hungry when you're spiritually constipated. *(Sorry for the potty talk...I have four boys, I may not know much, but I know poop.)*

|FIGHTING WORDS|: Our great desire is that you will keep on loving others as long as life lasts, in order to make certain that what you hope for will come true. Then you will not become spiritually dull and indifferent. Instead, you will follow the example of those who are going to inherit God's promises because of their faith and endurance. (Hebrews 6:11-12 NLT).

Have there been seasons in your life when you've used the Holy Spirit to accomplish your own agenda instead of actually having a relationship with Him? If you have children or just someone you really, really love, can you imagine them only coming to you if they needed something from you or to clean up their mess? Wouldn't you long for them to just hug you or snuggle with you or tell you a joke or tell you they love you for no reason? It wouldn't be much of a relationship otherwise, and yet we do this all of the time to God.

IF you're hungry, ASK FOR MORE. The more of Him you get, the more you'll want. And here's the thing: He doesn't give us more of His heart, mind, Spirit so we can binge and sit on it and become spiritually obese. He gives us more than we need so we can overflow into the lives of our family and friends and co-workers and anyone else in our path. What would it look like for you to pour out His Spirit onto someone else today? Would it take shape in encouraging a friend, serving a neighbor, or going to war for someone in prayer? Just go for it and watch how it begins to change who you are for the better.

If you're not hungry for Him yet and don't really see the point of this ridiculously long chapter, don't worry! Call out the things that aren't as if they are. Ask yourself if you at least *want* to want more of Him in your life. No one can hold your hand through this. This is between you and God. This is the first step in having the scales drop from your eyes. Like what happened to Saul as God transformed Him and carried him from religion to relationship.

STOP and pray for God to help you want more of Him. Pray for Him to make you discontent with a life that is not drenched in Him. Ask Him for a verse to encourage and inspire you, then write it down and keep it someplace where you can see it always.

{Wonder in Suffering}

| FIGHTING WORDS |: That I may know him and the power of his resurrection, and may share in his sufferings, becoming like him in his death (Philippians 3:10 ESV).

One morning I met a friend for coffee in the wee hours before the sun came up. We went deep as we talked about the fury of God's love for us and ended our time together at The Journey Church for morning prayer. The verse above is what we arrived to that morning in their devotional. We wept and prayed together as we processed the enormity of the power of His resurrection and the importance of being willing to be present in His suffering.

As a culture, and as humans, we tend to hold suffering at arm length. We "do" things around suffering that look nice for others. We stand on it's edge, at times fighting it back with an emotional baseball bat. We want the glory and grace of the resurrection, we want the happy and the nice and the pretty that is born from Jesus' sacrifice, but we avoid the down and dirty trenches of suffering like the plague. We pray prayers of safety and protection, and sometimes we live in "Christian" bubbles as we guard our hearts from anything even remotely smelling of that ominous word: SUFFERING. The problem is, that time we spend running from it, guarding against it, and trying to protect our family from it, is wasting *valuable, earth-shaking* experiences with our mighty Creator. We want the victory without the messy, without the heartache, without the nakedness…but without risking these things we cannot truly *know the enormity* of His love for us. Can we truly soak and bask in His presence when we only want part of what He has to offer? Avoiding suffering keeps us from the fullness of knowing God and experiencing what HE has for our lives. Avoiding suffering keeps us from ever risking it all.

I don't mean to invite suffering or create it. Plenty of people thrive on creating their own drama, that's not what I'm talking about. I'm just saying when hard times come to your door—or your neighbor's—don't run away. See what happens. Nope, I'm not smoking crack. Seriously just try it.

In the depths of our family's "great depression," after two autism diagnoses and losing everything, I can honestly say we were at an all-time low. At first I was angry with God. We chased after every lead we could think of to get us out of the mess we were in. But slowly, as we began to accept what was happening, we saw it as an opportunity to draw close to God, and as we experienced and encountered God as our Provider, it changed us. That gut-wrenching season in our lives deepened us and cultivated a culture of hunger for Him that continues to grow today, and we would have missed it if we wouldn't have had the guts to press into the pain.

{The Road}

By late September of 2011, the Extreme Makeover crew had left, the dust began to settle on life after "reality" T.V., and I started to feel the pressure of outside expectations and I felt like I was going to crumble. One morning, as I drove up our driveway, I stopped at the barn at the bottom of our hill and just looked up at our beautiful new home. I sat there on that fall day and stared in a heavy amazement, asking God what had just happened. Not expecting an answer, I started to put my beat-up old van in drive. All of the sudden a thought went through my head: "You think this is amazing? You have no clue what else I have in store for you. This is just the beginning."

Just the beginning? Just the beginning? I had been showing my house non-stop to on lookers and people I felt like I couldn't say no to. I was exhausted and grouchy as I tried to keep a house, with three young boys, "tour ready." I felt like I had traded my life for a job as a tour guide in a museum. On top of that, I was drowning in guilt about those negative feelings toward such a huge gift.

A few weeks later, Lauren Cunningham, the founder of YWAM was sitting at our dining room table. We slicked up and smiled real nice like while we pretended to be the happy family people expected us to be 24/7. This sweet, tender, and amazingly compassionate man could see through the empty smiles though. He told us the story of how 30 years ago he and his wife had received a similar gift. Then he looked right at us and said, "Someday you will be truly grateful for this gift." I didn't get it. Did we not seem grateful?

Today, I know what he was talking about. It took us a couple of years to adjust to our new lives. To be able to balance giving back and making sure people know how grateful we are and actually protecting our family and the space our special boys need to thrive. I can honestly say there isn't a morning that passes that I don't look out my kitchen window and praise God for this enormous gift. Not just the incredible house, but also the massive gift of life and love and relationship it has brought.

I could have easily missed God's voice that morning in my driveway. I could have hauled butt back up to my routine as usual and missed that thought I know God gave me. I could have seen the build as a happy ending to a sad story, but in the silence of my minivan that autumn morning, God's voice brought me a hope so deep it took me years to understand. The house was just the beginning.

Lord open our eyes to the intense blessings of new beginnings.

{Wonder Guts}

My mom used to tell me God didn't speak to her. She would read and pray and be still and silent and then...NOTHING. One time at a Fight Night, my friend Lu was speaking and asked each of the women to take some quiet time and write down what they heard God saying to them.

I remember looking at the pink piece of paper in my mom's hand with two words written on it: *cat gut*. That's what my mom heard. We laugh about it all of the time now. When we ask God something and we don't think we hear anything we say "cat gut." [Family Disclaimer: If you think the preceding paragraph is more weird than funny, know that we recently discovered we're actually *that* weird family... it's not you, it's us.]

Here's the thing. God speaks to *all* of us. Could you imagine NOT wanting to talk to your own child? That's ridiculous! He's talking; we just have to realize that if we're not hearing Him, we might not be tuned to the right channel.

Maybe you've heard the illustration about God's voice being like radio waves. There's actually music going on all around us all of the time but we can only hear it when we turn the radio on and switch it to the right channel. God has always been speaking to you; you just have to find the right channel to find out what He's saying. You have to figure out how you hear Him and experience Him. The point is, a lot of us think God has just been silent when really we just don't realize how He's speaking to us and working around us.

For years I thought God only talked to the people in the Bible and maybe a chosen few here in this lifetime, but now I know we were designed for intimacy with Him and that means He speaks to all of us. Through a thought, through a song, through a picture or words on a page, His voice whispers and at times roars. His words birth life and adventure and love. He beckons us to find His frequency in our own lives. For whatever reason, I find that frequency the most when I'm mopping my floor. He's also whispered words as I folded clothes and scrubbed toilets. Other times, He's enchanted me with His love as I listen to my favorite Pandora station lying face down on my dirty kitchen floor. There are NO boundaries on his ability to communicate with His children.

{Shaken, Not Stirred}

Have you ever been stirred into complacency? Inspired just enough to get a warm, fuzzy feeling but not enough to actually propel you into your God-given destiny? Have you ever wanted more out of life and your relationship with God only to allow fear, safety and comfort lull you back into life as usual?

I'll just say it: I have. I've clung to the security of well-paying jobs over the freedom of following Jesus. I've white knuckled relationships with people over the daring whispers of an adventurous God because it was easier to just follow a "Moses" in my life and be spoon-fed someone else's experience than to pursue a personal connection with my Creator.

One warm spring morning, I was sitting on my patio reading and drinking coffee. I had envisioned a morning of serene intimacy with God and instead ended up sipping cold coffee while digesting partial Scripture and of course being interrupted by fighting kids and a screaming baby. After about the 15th time of getting up to stop a near stabbing and the baby from eating what I'm still hoping was dirt in the flower bed, I came back to a wind-blown Bible. On the pages now opened, I read something that changed me:

"For this is what the Lord of Heaven's Armies says: In just a little while I will again shake the heavens and the

earth, the oceans and the dry land. I will shake all the nations, and the treasures of all the nations will be brought to this Temple. I will fill this place with glory, says the Lord of Heaven's Armies. The silver is mine, and the gold is mine, says the Lord of Heaven's Armies. The future glory of this Temple will be greater than its past glory, says the Lord of Heaven's Armies. And in this place I will bring peace. I, the Lord of Heaven's Armies, have spoken!" (Haggai 2:6-9 NLT).

While we can ignore a stirring, a shaking from the Lord is something you can't recover from. A shaking comes when we're willing to come to Him, baggage in tow, and say, "I don't know what to do with this, and I'm sorry for trying to take care of it myself." And then we just let Him do His stuff; we allow ourselves to be vulnerable enough for Him to shake off all of us that was never meant to be.

When we picture being shaken, I think we imagine something furious or outrageous violently jolting us. While God's shaking can be grandiose at times, sometimes it can also be the simple whisper of His voice that fiercely yet gently shakes us to our core. It's the deep thunder of His roar speaking life into us that summons us to release all we were never meant to be.

Have you been shaken lately? Maybe you should ask Him to shake you like a good ol' fashion martini and see what happens. *Ahhh!* My guts crawl into my throat over things like this because something incredibly exciting is about to happen!

{Wonder Weeds}

Brennan Manning wrote, *"The decision to come out of hiding is our initiation rite into the healing ministry of Jesus Christ. It brings its own reward. We stand in the Truth that sets us free and live out the Reality that makes us whole." (Abba's Child, 30)*

I struggle with not being the one to get things done. When I see a problem, I want it fixed in as few steps as possible. When I think something should be done, I don't wait for someone to give me permission or to hold my hand; I just do it. This may sound bold and fearless, but sometimes it's really a cover for the occasionally awkward silence that comes when we release the control so we can sit in the precious wonder that is God.

One night my struggle between desperately wanting to experience more of God's presence and my need to control things collided. As I laid awake wondering what it was that seemed to be keeping me from the looking into God's face and soaking in His presence, I heard these words: *stop trying.* I wrestled with this for a few days. One does not just simply "stop trying." I was confused and a little frustrated thinking, "Hello, God. Have you met me?"

My senior year in high school I was the Star Farmer in my FFA Chapter. Yep, you read the right. I was on the state champion livestock judging team, I raised sheep and cattle and I wore my blue corduroy Oregon FFA jacket with pride. Wipe that smirk off your face; FFA is cooler than you think! Anyhoo, almost 20 years later, my farming roots still run deep, and I love that my family and I get to raise pastured pork and grow orchard grass hay.

This past summer, the drought hit us hard. Little rain and almost no irrigation left our hay crop stunted, dry, and overflowing with a noxious flowering weed called Queen Ann's Lace. This weed doesn't just keep to the hay fields either. My husband and I spent the better part of a weekend ridding our yard of this pretty yet pesky weed. In 100-degree heat, armed with shovels and our trusty O-Hoe, we dug as many of those suckers out as we could. In the dry clay soil, the shovel banged against the dirt as if I was trying to dig into a cement sidewalk. To be honest, when my husband wasn't looking, I just chopped off the tops of most of them, knowing they would grow back but happy that at least the outside of our house looked better for the time being. I noticed that the weeds growing where the sprinkler line was leaking had been saturated with water...and actually came out with ease. Seriously: in those places, the giant, monstrous, prickly, tree-sized weeds came out by the roots with almost no effort. (OK, we may have waited a bit too long to take care of our little landscaping problem.)

So why am I boring you with the story of my weeds? *Oh, I'll tell you why!* As I was pulling and straining—and, I confess, swearing a little at the overwhelming situation—I realized the weeds symbolized the sin and strongholds and bondage in my own life. Being a woman of action I had ALWAYS tried to rid myself of anything nasty or sinful, and much of the time without even asking God for help. Some of the sin that was particularly hard to deal with I would just chop off at the surface so it looked good on the outside, but still, the roots of anger, bitterness, and rebellion were growing deep inside of me. Some of the weeds I tried so hard to pull out left me with scars and it taught me something. It's only when I have allowed myself to come to God, exposed and vulnerable, when I have just let go of the control and let Him soak into every part of who I am that I have truly been set free from my struggles.

We all have weed problems. And the thing with weeds is: they really don't need that much water to grow. They can over take a crop or a yard in a matter of weeks—even days sometimes. Sometimes weeds even look good enough to pass as flowers. But all the while, they're cutting off life to the crops and plants that were originally intended to thrive in that place.

How does wonder fit into this? Wonder comes when we just stop trying and struggling so hard. When we stop settling for what has taken over and we start to yearn for the life-giving Water that sustains and grows and cultivates what was destined to be from the beginning. Even if what's holding you back is socially acceptable, it's not what He originally intended for you. Are you going to settle for a life of anything less than His wonder? Are you going to settle for pretty weeds when He created you to be passionate, beautiful, life-giving fruit? Please say no.

It's time to allow God to shake us out of our comfort zones. It's time to stop trying to be anything we're not. It's time to let go of the control and let God's Spirit overwhelm us to the point of no return. This is where creativity and adventure are born. This is where wonder gets its wings. This is where you realize you were born to soar!

ASK YOURSELF:
When was the last time you experienced God's wonder?

Is there something awkward/painful/hard you've been avoiding that would serve you to press into?

Are there broken parts of your life that need to be exposed so they can ultimately be healed?

Pray with me: Lord I long to be filled with your WONDER. Take everything off my agenda today. Burn the old wine skins I keep trying to refill and expect revival from. Refresh your Spirit in me. Give me fresh eyes to see you. Lord I'm hungry for more of you in my life today. I long to hear Your voice. Whisper something special into my ear, remind me who You created me to be.

SIX: THE EAST WIND

|FIGHTING WORDS|: "Then Moses raised his hand over the sea, and the lord opened up a path through the water with a strong east wind. The wind blew all that night, turning the seabed into dry land. So the people of Israel walked through the middle of the sea on dry ground, with walls of water on each side!" (Exodus 14:21-22 NLT)

During times of worship, I often hear new things from God. During one time in His presence, I heard this:

The East Wind is blowing, can you feel it? Can you see it? It's blowing God's Spirit and power into a people rich with words but empty of wonder.

The East Wind is smashing, crashing, and breaking, and as it passes it leaves an essence of awe and the heartbeat of our Creator. The East Wind is fierce. It's deep and bold and comes with a roar. It's the strength from within, a deep seed that God planted when He spoke us into existence. It's the power that causes storms to still and rivers to part. Marked by outrageous love and drenched with anointing, the East Wind is a storm that leaves you forever changed. The East Wind is in Him and from Him and is Him.

In beautifully terrifying freedom, the glory, blessing, abundance, adventure, grit, wonder, and breathless abandon of the East Wind beckons us, "Come deeper, and deeper still."

The East Wind, a mere breath of El Hakkavod (The God of Glory), holds back the Red Sea and it's mocking darkness and calls us tenderly to walk into our destiny.

The East Wind is blowing, Can you feel it?

What is the East Wind? What does it do in our lives? Well, let me lay it down with a few stories won'tcha.

{Courage in Vulnerability}

In Luke 8, there's a woman who had been bleeding for 12 years. Ok wait, take that in... the girl had been in a constant state of PMS for 12 YEARRRRS! Can we just take a moment of silence for that fact alone? Sister had some wicked menstrual problems. Anyway, back to Luke and this woman who had to have been in the worst state of desperate. When Jesus passed by, she reached through the throngs of people just to touch a piece of His garment. She was changed in an instant. Her vulnerable faith led her to great courage. Her courage led her to an encounter that healed her.

We can't have an encounter with Jesus and be the same. The problem is, we're too easily satisfied to just be in the crowd surrounding Him. All the while, He's hoping we'll reach out for Him and receive His touch. I love the Luke 8 lady something fierce. She was an outcast; she wasn't allowed to touch other people because she was considered unclean. But for one second, she had simply stopped caring what her culture said she was. In pushing through the crowd to touch Jesus, her actions announced: "I am not who you say I am, and He is everything He says He is."

When the East Wind blows in our lives, God is saying: "I am strong, and I've made you stronger than you think." He's inviting us into something we never dreamed possible. When the East Wind blows, we come to that pivotal moment when we declare with our lives that either Jesus is everything He says He is, or He is nothing at all.

Here's the amazing thing about the East Wind; it's actually *always* blowing. God's power is *always* surrounding us. It's whether we choose to encounter it and live in it that changes the ball game.

So, do you feel His East Wind blowing? You might answer, "Honestly, no," and that's OK! You don't have to feel it. It's there whether you feel it or not, just like He is speaking whether you're listening or not.

Here's something to think about: have you been more comfortable listening to the voice of fear and doubt? Think about that for a second. I think we all want to say: "of course not!" but if we're honest with ourselves and God, I think we have to admit that there are times it just feels safer to listen to the whispers and lies. It's easier to believe the voice telling us we're insignificant and under-qualified, than to wake up to the reality that God wants us to bring heaven to earth every day and live in His powerful, life-giving presence.

It's easier to talk about the East Wind, to sing about it, to read about it, and to agree with it than it is let it move in us every day. But what would today look like if you just let the power of God in? If you stripped off the paralyzing lies and need for security and safety and just said: "OK, Lord: do your thing and I'll go where You lead me." That sounds good. You may even say those very words in your morning prayer, but what about when He leads you into the messiness of life? When He takes you somewhere inconvenient? What about when He leads you to risk it all? What about when He leads you to not only forgive, but to bless and love people in your life who have betrayed or maybe even abused you? What then? When we get to those roadblocks, we like to give biblical justification for why God surely wouldn't lead us "there." We build a wall that shields us from the glorious freedom, wonder and majesty that is the East Wind.

Today, I challenge you to ask God to destroy the walls you've built for protection and prepare to live the invigorating revival that comes with encountering God's mighty power.

{A God We Can't Control}

Do you ever wonder when your life is going to begin? Do you lay awake at night wondering when God is going to bring the dreams deep inside of you to reality? I can't even count the nights I've been kept up by worry and longing, wondering if He's really big enough to deliver what He's deposited deep inside of me. And then—here's the clincher—He starts to deliver, but I don't exactly like the package my promise comes in, or the timing, or the "delivery guy." Sometimes, I want to "help" God out a bit.

That, my friends, is exhausting. We need to long for a God we can't control?

Allowing God's Spirit to move through us freely is the difference between just not dying (the exhausting part) and actually living.

With four young boys in tow 24/7, the quote that's never far from my mind is, "Adventures are rarely fun while you're having them." My husband doesn't agree but as the mom, primary caregiver, and chief butt wiper I have to say it feels true a lot of the time.

I think most of the time the thoughts that run through our heads go something like this: "When_____ happens, THEN I will _____." We look at our lives as an accumulation of destinations when in reality, it is in the waiting, in the trenches, and in the everyday that heaven surrounds us. And we often need to surrender our idea of what that process will look like.

Singer Stephanie Gretzinger from Bethel Music did a video to promote her album *The Undoing.* In it she shares a conversation she had with God when He said to her, "All of this life is the undoing, until one day you'll be face to face with me and you'll be completely undone." Stephanie said she realized that all of life is a process, and His pleasure over her life was in her process. The promise land was in the middle of the journey — not at the end.

When we only look to the next thing, when we only dream as far as we see ourselves, when we white knuckle life and our need safety and answers and security, we miss out on so much of the process. It's in our undoing that letting go feels like freedom and smells like Jesus.

{Shaping Your Destiny}

Bill Johnson said, "Who we say we are is a prophetic declaration of how we will let God work through us." When I heard this, it wrecked me for a few days. It made me realize I had allowed years of labels and lies define who I was, instead of genuinely seeking out who HE created me to be.

I had let this kind of junk define me: "You're a community college drop out; you're not smart enough to write a book." "You're 30 pounds overweight—maybe you used to be beautiful, but now you're invisible." "Your house is always dirty, so not only are you not smart enough to contribute to society, but you're also bad wife and mother."

Yep, that's been my mental dialogue for years. No wonder it's taken so long to break free from the lies and believe I'm worth so much more to God than I could ever fathom.

|FIGHTING WORDS|: Set me as a seal upon your heart, a seal upon your arm, for love is strong as death, jealousy is fierce as the grave. It's flashes are flashes of

fire, the very flame of the Lord" (Song of Solomon 8:6 ESV).

What we allow to label us is who we're saying we are. Some labels seem harmless, but each label filters out a little more of our true selves. It's only when we are labeled by Him and for Him that we can even begin to taste the purpose He longs to bring to our lives.

If He's not the seal over your heart, what is? Your failures, your successes, your fears, the lies spoken over you? What defines you? What makes you who you are?

Didn't we already go over this in the chapter about identity? Yes, yes we did, but it's so very important that you know, I'm going to speak these God labels over you:

YOU ARE BEAUTIFUL

YOU ARE POWERFUL

YOU ARE SMART

YOU ARE INTERESTING

YOU ARE COURAGEOUS

YOU ARE DARING

YOU ARE SIGNIFICANT

YOU ARE WORTH IT

Who you say you are determines EVERYTHING about how you live, how you face your fears, and the size of mountains you'll let Him use you to move. It's time to rip off those old labels. It might be painful. Some of the labels might be stuck to you like a badly inked tattoo. You can't remove them by yourself. Ask Him right now to soak you with His Spirit. Ask God to start lifting off the labels of who you thought you were and replacing them with permanent seals of who HE says you are. Your life will change, but when you follow Him, it has to.

Get ready: He's got so much to say to you about how much He adores you, about how proud of you He is, and how He has amazing things in store for you when you're ready to let go and say yes!

{My Greatest Fear}

One time I lead an all-night prayer retreat. Twelve of us met at my church, loaded into a 15-passenger van, and set out to canvas our little valley with mountain-moving prayer. As someone who is in her jammies and asleep by 8:30 most nights, I knew pulling an all-nighter was going to be a challenge in itself. Armed with lots of coffee and snacks I got to the church early to prepare for the fearless brood of women, *aka the only friends I could find crazy enough to join me.*

Oh, did I mention I'm afraid of the dark? Yes I am. Ridiculously so. I arrived to our church, which was situated in an old outlet mall at the time. I unlocked the front door and had to get to the far backside of the building to turn the stinking lights on without being hacked to pieces by the ax murderer I was sure was waiting for me. Good news: no ax murderer... I made it to the light switch. I set the light dimmer, turned on the battery-operated candles, and started some soft music to get us in the prayin' mood. In the midst of the preparations, I felt like God was telling me to get on my face and just be still. But I kept going, sure it wasn't God and even more sure if it was God, He obviously didn't know how much I had to get done.

Again, I felt the urgency to get down on my face. Again, I ignored it. Yep, you heard it here first, I said no to God. TWICE. The truth is I was afraid. What if I stopped and something happened? Almost immediately that fear was overshadowed with: "what if I stop, get down on my face, and NOTHING happens?" I was afraid He would show up in a way that I wasn't comfortable with, and I was even more afraid He wouldn't show up at all. Guess what happened? *Nothing.* Yeah, nothing tends to happen when we skip over those little moments on our journey so we can hurry to reach our destination.

I don't know what would have happened that night had I stopped and experienced God and just worshiped Him. I know He showed up anyway because, well, He's God... He always shows up. But what I think I missed out on was a bit of intimacy with Him, a moment He had reserved for just the two of us. Even now it makes me wonder: what else am I skipping over, masking it with the lie that I'm too busy when really I'm just afraid of what will happen if I say yes and make a move toward Him?

Are you afraid? Have you stopped moving toward a dream and masked it with the lie that you're just too busy? Or maybe you've just convinced yourself it's not really your dream anymore. Fear thrives and grows and multiplies in the dark. But guess what? When we can own it—when we can come to God and say honestly, "I'm just afraid"—He will bring us to a greater awareness of who He is. His love casts the fear out, and the deeper we're connected to Him, the more willing we are to say yes to Him in the face of uncertainty, risk, and the ever-dreaded disapproval of others.

There's no shame in being afraid. Honestly! But don't sit around in it; fear is the graveyard for dreams and the birthplace of regret. Bring fear to light, admit it, and then leave it. It will creep back up, but when it does, you just have to ask God for the covering and the strength to kick it in the teeth and move on because NOTHING is impossible with God. NOTHING!

Adidas wrote this marketing campaign about the impossible, and while it's not necessarily spiritual, it's one of the most spiritual things I've ever read:

"Impossible is just a big word thrown around by small men who find it easier to live in the world they've been given than to explore the power they have to change it. Impossible is not a fact, it's an opinion. Impossible is not a declaration, it's a dare. Impossible is potential. Impossible is temporary. Impossible is nothing."

| *FIGHTING WORDS:* | *Jesus looked at them and said, "With man this is impossible, but with God all things are possible"* (Matthew 19:26 ESV).

It's time to stop saying we believe nothing is impossible with God; it's time to start actually living it! Are you ready? What's your impossible?

What do you need to let go of? What do you need undone in your life? It's in the challenges and failures, victories and breakthrough that our stories are written. Can you fathom letting God be God? No really, think about that question? Can you fathom it? Because if your answer is yes it means you're ready to put feet to what you say you believe. If the answer is yes, you're ready to let God out of the box you've put Him in. Adventure and freedom happen when we surrender and say, "Now it's your turn God."

PRAY WITH ME: Lord I long for the impossible today. I want to experience You in a new way. Show me what that looks like.

SEVEN: WAR

|FIGHTING WORDS|: For God doesn't give us a spirit of fear and timidity, but of power, love and self-discipline." (2 timothy 1:7 NLT).

One night C.J. and I were talking with some friends about the spiritual revival that had taken place in our lives, and it made me start thinking about exactly what had changed in me. What was the breaking point for breakthrough? There was a miscarriage and then another miscarriage in a matter of months, friend drama, home drama, me drama…*lots of drama*. There were people speaking into my life and lots of self-reflection. I think all of these things contributed to the change, but they didn't make the change, they didn't bring revival.

Revival came when I acknowledged that this journey is a battle I was willing to fight. *What does that even mean?* For me fighting means a lot of things, but probably none of them are what you would think. If love is the greatest weapon in our arsenal, then in order to use it we have to know who we are; we have to be secure in who He made us to be. If the enemy is defeated by the blood of the Lamb and the POWER of our testimony (Rev 12:11), we have to be willing to be real and raw and vulnerable: sharing who we are and what we've been through so that others can experience the power of His victory.

I realized that to have real breakthrough and serious transformation there could be no more sitting around waiting for life to happen to me. God showed me that HIS is an anointed fight, HIS is a battle we should all be up for, because HIS is the fight that He has ordained for us all, from the beginning. THE FIGHT, THE WAR, THE BATTLE is to be secure in who we are so that we can love others so outrageously it calls even the hardest of people into their God-given destiny!

Don't mistake the weapon of love as something flowery, easy, or weak. This love is forged in the battlefield, shaped in struggle, and refined only by Jesus' resurrection power. It's fiery and fierce, it goes beyond the boundaries of man-made religion, and it breaks down the barriers of self-preservation. It takes a warrior's heart and a Father's love to wage a war of this caliber. Whether you know it or not, He created you uniquely, intentionally and without mistake to be a mighty Kingdom warrior. The battle is raging, love is needed, are you willing?

|FIGHTING WORDS|: For we are not fighting against flesh-and-blood enemies, but against evil rulers and authorities of the unseen world, against mighty powers in this dark world, and against evil spirits in the heavenly places. (Ephesians 6:11-13 NLT).

Here 's another passage that came to me during a time of worship:

There are places in life where only love can go and come out alive. Scary places filled with the unknown. Hurting places that we pack away tightly, so no one can damage that tender part again.

In the deep recesses of hurt and betrayal, in the dark hidden corners of scandals past and pains that seem unforgivable, it feels like nothing can heal and "beauty from ashes" might as well be a fairy tale. It's in these cavernous, lonely places filled with shame and fear and condemnation that only love can breakthrough and begin to rebuild something beautiful out of the rubble. LOVE CAN REVIVE.

There are times when only our weathered scars can bring life back to someone who can't see hope. The stories that weave our lives together, the memories that haunt us, and the days we may long to forget are what give us the authority to breathe life to the dead, to heal the sick and broken hearted, and to set the prisoners free.

We are tempted to hide. We are tempted to cover and try to forget. But life is unleashed and love is abundant when we can own our stories and let God transform them into movements instead of chains of bondage.

When there is no more hiding, no more covering up, no more protecting, no more loving with an agenda, we encounter love on a new level. This experience of breathing life from pain and calling the broken into their destinies is called war. War is where love lives. It's like no war we've seen or read about. No, this kind of war only comes with surrender, long suffering, joy, courage, and victory — all drenched in love and discovered in grace.

War can wreck you in the most glorious way. War keeps relationship first and doesn't need rules to know how to live. War seeks His voice first. War longs to be filled — no, overflowed — with the Spirit of God. War cannot be duplicated by self; war can only be lived out when God is our breath, our hunger, our identity. This war is HIS, and for HIM. Are you ready? Are you willing?

| *FIGHTING WORDS* |: *The Spirit of the Lord God is*

upon me, because the Lord has anointed me to bring good news to the poor; he has sent me to bind up the brokenhearted, to proclaim liberty to the captives, and the opening of the prison to those who are bound; to proclaim the year of the Lord's favor, and the day of vengeance of our God; to comfort all who mourn; to grant to those who mourn in Zion – to give them a beautiful headdress instead of ashes, the oil of gladness instead of mourning, the garment of praise instead of a faint spirit; that they may be called oaks of righteousness, the planting of the Lord, that he may be glorified" (Isaiah 61:1-3 ESV).

{The Sandwich}

When we encounter love in its truest form, it heals us. It transforms us.

My friend Heather has an incredible story about how a sandwich saved her marriage. Yep, two slices of bread and some processed meat became the turning point for her and her husband. At a time when their relationship was so rocky she didn't even want to look at him, much less serve him, she made him a sandwich. In the throes of intense marital strife, when her husband was angry and Heather felt done, God told her to make him a sandwich...so she did. Still hurt and confused and fuming, she slapped that sandwich down on the table and walked away. He didn't say thank you. He didn't seem grateful. But that night, the mood of their relationship shifted. God used something little and seemingly insignificant to start a healing process that changed everything.

After hearing Heather's story, a friend and I wrote "sandwich" on our wrists to remind us that little acts of love and surrender can make a big difference to the men we chose to spend our lives with.

My husband and I have been married 14 years. They have been 14 of the most amazingly, terrible, adventurous, heart-wrenching, beautifully chaotic years of our lives. We've had seasons of tremendous blessing and we've had seasons of mind-blowing struggle. If I'm being honest, there have been times when I wondered if we were going to make it. Why? Because it's hard to live and serve and care for another person who is just as messed up as I am.

It's hard to make time for sex and romance with kids popping up at all of the wrong times. It's hard to trust after bad things have happened. It's hard to forgive when hearts have been broken. It's hard to love like Jesus because a lot of us come into a relationship broken and with years of baggage. Here's what I know though; when the "D" word isn't an option, when walking away from hard relationships isn't an option, things get messy and real, and we have to deal with our hurt. But when we hold on, the other side of the struggle reveals something real and deep and imperfectly beautiful. Sometimes, healing seems impossible. Sometimes, it's a simple as a sandwich.

Disclaimer: This concept obviously doesn't apply to abusive relationships, and please know from the bottom of my heart this is in NO WAY SHAPE OR FORM me judging you if you've had a divorce. It's just my experience with my man.

{Just Shut Up & Love}

|FIGHTING WORDS|: Love suffers long and is kind; love does not envy; love does not parade itself, is not puffed up; does not behave rudely, does not seek its own, is not provoked, thinks no evil; does not rejoice in iniquity, but rejoices in the truth; bears all things, believes all things, hopes all things, endures all things. Love never fails. But whether there are prophecies, they will fail; whether there are tongues, they will cease; whether there is knowledge, it will vanish away.
 (1 Corinthians 13:4-8 NKJV).

I was talking to my mom a while ago, asking her advice on a friendship I was struggling with. Wait, let me just say: what I really wanted was for her to agree with me and protect her baby girl.

Her answer caught me off guard, "I think God wants you to shut up and just love." *Yeaaahhhh*, that was NOT the answer I was hoping for. "Shut up and just love" pretty much sums up 80% of the New Testament.

Offended? Hurt? Angry? Bitter? Entitled? We allow our emotion and our own baggage to cloud Jesus' message: LOVE. LOVE. LOVE. Oh and when you're done with that. LOVE. He doesn't just stop there though. There are so many verses telling us *how* to do it. We can't cry victim and say we don't know how. We can't claim ignorance because He spells it out. Oh yeah: and He lived it. Beaten, spit on, abused, publicly slandered, yet still, HE LOVED. He loved the unexpected, the prostitutes, the drunks, and the socially scorned. He hung out with them when to do so was sealing the deal on how much the religious leaders of the day would hate Him. Ahhhh! I LOVE this man. I want to be just like Him, and as I search for a way to do that, my mom's words echo in my head. "Shut up and just love."

| *FIGHTING WORDS* | : "*If your enemies are hungry, feed them. If they are thirsty, give them something to drink.*" (Romans 12:20 NLT).

"*Always be humble and gentle. Be patient with each other, making allowances for each other's faults because of your love. Make every effort to keep yourselves united in the spirit, binding yourselves together with peace. FOR THERE IS ONE BODY and ONE SPIRIT, just as*

you have been called to one glorious hope for the future."
(Ephesians 4:2-4 NLT).

In other words, just shut up and love! Sometimes it's downright painful. We think we're right, and others should think like us. We want to love how *we* want to love, but it's not always the kind of love Jesus intended. We have been hurt, so we are justified in not forgiving and not loving right? After all, you have no clue what kind of monster that person is. But Jesus is our example, and when life got gritty and disgusting and unbearably hard, through the power of the Holy Spirit, He forgave. He loved.

I'm just now coming to terms with some abuses that happened long ago. It's been a dark spot lodged in my guts, a place I felt justified in not surrendering to God because I was entitled to my anger and rage over what had been taken from me. It has plagued my relationships and even parts of my marriage; it was a shadow cast by someone I had not forgiven because I thought I didn't have to. But my inability to forgive empowered the enemy to create doubt and fear and an overall lack of trust in anyone—even God at times.

As I started the process of love and forgiveness, chains began breaking, light began shattering darkness, and love began its victory. That process feels so huge and impossible, and honestly it can only be done through a constant drenching of His Spirit and presence. It's so stinking hard, but He never says it won't be; He just says to trust Him. As I pray blessing on this person (yep, you read that right, BLESS the person you're trying to forgive), the fruit of the Holy Spirit pours out. (For more on forgiveness check out our STRIKE Manifesto at www.fightingforward.com.)

Thank you Lord. It's time to stop talking. It's time to shut up and just love.

|*FIGHTING WORDS*|:*"Don't just pretend to love others. Really love them. Hold tightly to what is good. Love each other with genuine affection, and take delight in honoring each other."* (Romans 12:9-10 NLT).

{The Ministry of Life}

The other day, while returning an email, I told a friend that God had called me into full-time women's ministry. I shuttered as I typed those words and quickly erased them...and here's why. At the first retreat I ever hosted, a woman asked me a question: "I guess my dream would be to have a vineyard with my husband, but is that ok...you know, that my dream isn't ministry?" She asked this right before I had to get people ready for lunch so I quickly answered, "Of course! Everything we do has an impact on the Kingdom." I anguished over that hurried response for a week, wishing I would have forgotten about the logistics of getting a horde of women in the lunch line. I wish I would have told her to "go for it" because God had given her that dream, and He would use it to extend the tent pegs of His kingdom. *(And also I just really like wine.)*

Here's the thing, *wait for it...*we are all called to ministry...you are called to ministry. Un-bunch your panties, it's true.

We are all, in fact, called to women's ministry, to children's ministry, to men's ministry, to feeding the homeless and giving to the poor. But guess what? It's not called ministry it's called LIFE.

Whether you're a lawyer, a stay-at-home mom, a nurse, or a farmer, WE ARE ALL CALLED to work for the good of the Kingdom! We are *not* called to compartmentalize "work," "family," "friends," and "God." Sometimes I think the label of "ministry" makes the masses feel justified in *not* living a life purposefully devoted to Kingdom work because "ministry" is meant for those with a special calling set apart from "real" life. Insert giant, annoying buzzer here. WRONG.

If you have decided to love Jesus, guess what? You are automatically inducted into the *ministry of life.* It's weird how words can unintentionally create barriers. If I don't label what I do as ministry, but rather as life, is it any less important? It feels less important, but that's called pride, and that's my own issue. When someone asks what I do, what do I tell them? "Well, I wipe butts and occasionally do dishes. Oh, and I love to cheer women on..." How do I classify what God has called me to without the label of "ministry"? Does it even matter? There's a bit of seductiveness in the word ministry, somehow implying ministry is a program that I sacrifice for—something that only really spiritual people can be a part of.

Not long ago, I saw a guy from our pastoring days (or should I say, the days we were employed by a church.) Knowing that my hubby now works for a hospital system and no longer a church or "official" ministry, the man asked, "Does C.J. miss being in ministry?"

I said, "Not really, because our lives are ministry." I don't think this guy meant anything by his question necessarily, but it made my blood boil. Just a few weeks before at work, C.J. had been called to anoint a hospital patient with oil and pray for healing because the chaplain was busy. This is life. Is it less ministry because C.J. works for a "secular" organization? As bosses and employees, as mothers and wives and daughters, as patrons at a restaurant or shoppers at Target, every second of everyday we are called to move the Kingdom forward and to LOVE others by using the gifts God has given us...hmmhmm: M-I-N-I-S-T-R-Y!

Paul was a tent maker by day and still managed to blaze as an apostle, preacher, teacher, and healer by living ministry. This is in NO WAY a dig to those in paid full time "ministry." We should support great people and organizations that spread the Gospel. This is, however, a call to step out of complacency just because we don't bear an official label of "such and such" ministry. We are all called to work together. We are all a part of the body of Christ! When we no longer default to just letting the "pros" handle it, when we no longer hide behind the great excuse of being "unqualified," when we stop sitting back and expecting a chosen few to do 99% of the work, we will realize we are the workers...we are the leaders...we are the mountain movers!

|FIGHTING WORDS|: *When I called, you answered me; you made me bold and stouthearted. May all the kings of the earth praise you, O LORD, when they hear the words of your mouth. May they sing of the ways of the LORD, for the glory of the LORD is great. Though the LORD is on high, he looks upon the lowly, but the proud he knows from afar. Though I walk in the midst of trouble, you preserve my life; you stretch out your hand against the anger of my foes, with your right hand you save me. The LORD will fulfill [his purpose] for me; your love, O LORD, endures forever--do not abandon the works of your hands.* (Psalm 138:3-8 NIV).

I love Psalm 138; it sounds so gritty and raw. He made us bold and stouthearted. Some days it doesn't feel like it though. Some days it feels like I'm going to break at the next "thing" that punches me in the guts. But He made us strong and bold to endure, to press on.

Today, don't back down. Don't shy away. He's created you for more. You're a fighter: a stouthearted, gritty creation filled with boldness and gumption because He put all of that in you. Own it. Swim around in this thought until your fingers get all prune-y. Decide what kind of warrior you were designed to be and then go after it, charging forward with your love as your weapon, your shield, and your motivation.

{Yahweh Cover Me}

|FIGHTING WORDS|: "O Lord, my Lord, the strength of my salvation, you have covered my head in the day of battle." (Psalm 140:7 ESV).

Here's a problem with war and warring for people; all too often we join the fight full of passion and ideals, but somewhere in the process we forget that the power and victory belong to God. Sometimes we invite God to come along for the ride, but then we rush in unprotected and uncovered. When we're not drenched in Him—His love, grace, and mercy—things can go south quite quickly. We can start inserting our own opinions of people and situations, we can react out of hurt and anger, or worse, we can tear down, divide, and dishearten the very people we're supposed to build up.

I've done it. I'm sure if you're honest you have too. One time a friend came to me broken and about to make a huge life decision I didn't agree with. I had been hurt by lots of stuff throughout our friendship that I had never dealt with, and while my words were, "I'll fight for you in this." My heart meant: "I'm going to push my agenda on you because you're wrong and I'm still mad at you." I zeroed in on the "huge mistake" I thought she was about to make, and, armed with lots of brokenness and anger and being fluent in christianese, I commenced my assault. For the Glory of God, of course.

Here's the thing: when humanness wants to expose and call out ugly, we become ugly. God's heart is always restoration, always love, always grace and forgiveness. I alienated a friend because I was hurt when what God actually wanted from me was to remind her of who she is and to call her as He sees her. You may disagree with this, but it's the truth: the war He's asks us to wage is one of love and redemption.

I had to own up to this. I had to ask forgiveness and it wasn't easy. Is there someone you need to ask forgiveness from? No, no, no, this isn't a time to drudge up all of the junk they did, this isn't the part where you get to justify being legalistic because [fill in the blank]. Right now can you think of someone God probably wanted you to call up instead of calling out, but out of your own pain, insecurity, or fear you decided to be the authority on what their life should look like? Apologizing may not change anything, but it might change everything. He covers us with Him so even when it feels unfair, even when it hurts and downright sucks we can see others through His eyes. When we're able to war for another person we're saying: I see you, I love you, and THIS is who you are! It's not pretty, it's war. And whether you think so or not you are a warrior.

Where are the places only love can go in your life? Who has God given you to WAR for?

Has anyone ever WARRED for you? How did it change you?

Have you ever WARRED for someone who is really hard to love? (Be honest with yourself.) Where is that relationship now?

Have you ever WARRED for someone WITHOUT an agenda and without expecting ANYTHING in return?

If you haven't, today your challenge is to pray for God to reveal someone in your life WHO NEEDS TO BE

WARRED FOR. Ask Him what that looks like and how to start.

[A NOTE ON HEARING FROM GOD:] Hearing His voice is about relationship; it's not binding the unexplainable into pre-determined steps. Trust and believe that He loves you, He created you, and He *is* speaking to you!

PRAY WITH ME: Lord open my eyes to how you want me to war for you. Seep down into the deepest parts of where I'm harboring unforgiveness, bitterness, anger, jealousy, pride, or religion. I confess these things to you and ask you to destroy them and replace them with LOVE, joy, peace patience, kindness, goodness, gentleness, and self-control. Keep my eyes focused on you as I fight. Remind me today what I'm fighting for.

EIGHT: RISKY BUSINESS

{When the Church Hobbles into a Bar}

When I started Fight Nights at my house, I had no clue what they would turn into or even where we would meet after the warm summer nights that allowed us to meet outside on our hill were gone. I felt like God just wanted me to host and take it one month at a time. I didn't know what it would look like, but I knew it had to be something different, something freeing, somewhere that anyone could come with any past, at any phase of their spiritual journey, and be comfortably uncomfortable.

The first night came and it was beautiful. I didn't decorate unless you count mowing down the knee-high weeds. I wanted something with no frills or distractions, something that was just real and simple. God used my YES and in spite of my fumbled words, (I'm not exaggerating, at one point I said fart instead of smart), He worked powerfully in the lives of women there that night. Women came who would never step foot in a church. Women came from all different denominations around our valley, crying out with the same heart and worshipping and praying together. That night changed me and showed me that walking forward and saying yes has nothing to do with our abilities and everything to do with allowing God's power to shine through our weaknesses.

Three months later as the group continued to grow I realized two things. The first was: I didn't really know how to categorize what a Fight Night was. It was more than a bible study; it was women speaking of the victory God had in their lives. By making Revelations 12:11 the heartbeat of our group, through sharing and being authentic and transparent women were being set free. I didn't want these nights to end up being a Bible lesson and a good worship set, so the strict guideline for anyone sharing was that it had to be their story. I knew if Fight Night became a soap box or platform for women to just get up and talk about things we should or shouldn't do, it would turn stale and we were all too hungry for God to let it come to that. *(Remember the power of the testimony?)*

The second thing I realized was we were going to need a place to meet for the winter. I didn't want to go to a church; I wanted something with ambiance, somewhere beautiful without trying to be beautiful.

After putting a desperate plea out on Facebook a friend suggested a place called Havana Republic. They had an upstairs room that could easily house over 100 people, and it was right downtown. The old brick interior was highlighted by a disco ball and some sort of adult dancy swing, Oh; did I forget to mention this room doubles as one of the hottest night clubs in town on the weekends? We were only a couple of weeks out, and I still hadn't found a place big enough to accommodate our group, so one day in late fall I met my husband at the upstairs room on his lunch hour. Before we met my friend Amy, who was giving us a tour, C.J. and I stood out on Main Street in front of the building and just prayed that God would make it very clear to us if THIS was the place.

We walked up the stairs that opened up into an amazingly GORGEOUS upper room. At the same exact time we both knew *this was it*. As Amy started to tell us about the place, we found out they were slow during the week and this room sat empty so they would let us use it for FREE because the women coming would bring in business. They made a special menu for us and gave us our own waitress.

It's called the Bohemian Club now, but it's become our home and it will continue to be as long as they let us. While some people don't come because of its location I have so many who actually DO come because of it. Every month I hear someone say some version of this statement, "Any church that meets in a bar is my kind of church." Fight Nights certainly aren't for everyone, and I get that and it's OK.

I was so nervous to announce where we were meeting because frankly I had already come against some pretty strong opposition from women in our community who didn't like how God was leading me to lead. It was hurtful and disheartening and I almost quit. It was uncomfortable to have people who didn't know me and hadn't even come to the event, tear me down and gossip and, yes, even turn me into their pastor.

I don't share this to stir up drama or to say poor me, I say this because if you say YES to God you can't stop or quit or even pause for every well meaning (or not so well-meaning) person who criticizes what you know God is calling you to, or you will NEVER do anything. Being fearless isn't just doing the bold, unconventional, underground stuff that God calls you to because it's popular or trendy or edgy. Being fearless is saying yes to God one step at a time even in the face of people not liking you, gossiping about you and using their own fears and insecurities to try to limit your beliefs too. Yes, that kind of response can hurt. Being fearless is being able to keep moving forward in love but without picking up other people's baggage and without becoming a complete witch to the dart throwers.

The truth is almost no one wants to actually pray for the people making their life hell, but when we do we're telling them, "I see you, and this isn't you, and God is helping me love you like He loves you."

If we let naysayers—or people who just don't understand what God is doing—offend us, if we can't take criticism by looking at ourselves and asking God if there's any truth to it and moving on, then bitterness and resentment will overshadow us and outshine any good we think we are doing. The moment we allow offense or hurt feelings to direct us, we are telling God that our emotions outweigh His purpose. Being fearless isn't plowing over anyone who disagrees with us, it's having the courage to ask God what He says and then willfully choosing to love and forgive and call up anyone who is trying to stifle His Spirit in you.

{Permission: You Don't Need It}

Did you know that you don't need permission to be who God created you to be? Hold on to your panties girls because guess what? You don't even need permission to DO the things God has called you/created you/designed you to do. You know that thing way down deep? The thing you've dreamed about and planned in your head a thousand times? He gave you that dream, and He doesn't just *want* you to follow Him and move forward toward that dream... He expects you to.

| FIGHTING WORDS |: "So I say to you, ask, and it will be given to you; seek, and you will find; knock, and it will be opened to you. For everyone who asks receives, and he who seeks finds, and to him who knocks it will be opened. If a son asks for bread from any father among you, will he give him a stone? Or if he asks for a fish, will he give him a serpent instead of a fish? Or if he asks for an egg, will he offer him a scorpion? If you then, being evil, know how to give good gifts to your children, how much more will your heavenly Father give the Holy Spirit to those who ask Him!" (Luke 11:9-13 NIV).

I think sometimes we wait to do things until some authority figure says we can or should or until they hold our hands and show us how. But when God births something inside of us, when *HE* asks us to start that business, or write that book, or host that small group, *HE* expects us to move forward even if we feel overwhelmed and under-qualified.

READ Nehemiah 2:12-20 (NLT):

I slipped out during the night, taking only a few others with me. I had not told anyone about the plans God had put in my heart for Jerusalem. We took no pack animals with us except the donkey I was riding. After dark I went out through the Valley Gate, past the Jackal's Well, and over to the Dung Gate to inspect the broken walls and burned gates. Then I went to the Fountain Gate and to the King's Pool, but my donkey couldn't get through the rubble. So, though it was still dark, I went up the Kidron

Valley instead, inspecting the wall before I turned back and entered again at the Valley Gate.

The city officials did not know I had been out there or what I was doing, for I had not yet said anything to anyone about my plans. I had not yet spoken to the Jewish leaders – the priests, the nobles, the officials, or anyone else in the administration. But now I said to them, "You know very well what trouble we are in. Jerusalem lies in ruins, and its gates have been destroyed by fire. Let us rebuild the wall of Jerusalem and end this disgrace!" Then I told them about how the gracious hand of God had been on me, and about my conversation with the king.

They replied at once, "Yes, let's rebuild the wall!" So they began the good work.

But when Sanballat, Tobiah, and Geshem the Arab heard of our plan, they scoffed contemptuously. "What are you doing? Are you rebelling against the king?" they asked.

I replied, "The God of heaven will help us succeed. We, his servants, will start rebuilding this wall. But you have no share, legal right, or historic claim in Jerusalem."

Nehemiah knew he had to rebuild the temple. He got permission from the King (which actually could have cost him his life), and he set out. He didn't ask anyone else's opinion; he didn't need validation or someone to walk him through how to do this seemingly impossible job. He took a few guys, snuck out at night, and didn't tell anyone of his plans. He scoped it out on the down low. And even after he revealed his plans and people scoffed and laughed and told him he was crazy, he kept moving forward.

We've been given permission from our king to move forward; in fact, He died so we could be set free to do so. He left us with a "helper" called the Holy Spirit (John 14:26). We read Scriptures and listen to speakers all of the time telling us that we are created for something and we all have gifts, and then we move on like somehow it doesn't apply to us. Or maybe we post it on Facebook or proclaim it to our friends, waiting for feedback, waiting for encouragement when really He has given all that we need to just go.

Sometimes we treat our relationship with Jesus like it's only a one way ticket to eternity and we sit here on our thumbs in survival mode, but hey, at least we're going to heaven right? That thought process used to make me furious but now it just sparks a fire in me to carry a life altering message: You were built for more. He wants us to bring a little heaven to earth. He longs for us to tap into the glory He's left us with and guess what? We're supposed to unpack that gift in THIS lifetime.

But what if I fail? What if my friends and family don't understand? What if I don't know what I'm doing? Awesome! That's what faith is for. You may fail; I've failed so many times I've lost track. I've failed businesses and lost everything. I had to move in with my parents for nine months with three kids, all seeming failures.

We hit bottom so hard that a month before my 30th birthday, I sat in the DHS waiting room to apply for food stamps. I still get nervous at the checkout counter wondering if my debit card will be denied even though I know we now have money to pay for food. That was rough—probably the roughest time in our lives—but I wouldn't change it for the world. God used that "failure" not only to draw me closer to Him but also to set the stage for the next phase of our lives, which has been an "Extreme" gift to say the least.

We can't progress in our relationship with God, and we can't fully discover who we were created to be if we aren't willing to risk. If strength is birthed through brokenness, risk is a win/win situation.

I sliced the top of my finger clean off a while ago. We're not talking a little slice of skin either; it hurt for a long time. It's so stupid, but that missing fingertip slowed me down and kept me from so much I needed to accomplish. You don't realize how much you use it until in its place is a painful, oozing scab. And can I just say; it's time for us to stop being painful oozing scabs in the body of Christ. There will no doubt be cynics and people who want to bring their version of reality to your door. People might flat out tell you that you can't or laugh at you just like the people in Nehemiah's story laughed at him and told him it couldn't be done. This stuff isn't for the faint of heart, but then again we weren't saved for a life of faintheartedness; we were redeemed for a life with a heart powered by the Holy Spirit.

Read 1 Corinthians 12:12-26 (MSG):

The human body has many parts, but the many parts make up one whole body. So it is with the body of Christ. Some of us are Jews, some are Gentiles, some are slaves, and some are free. But we have all been baptized into one body by one Spirit, and we all share the same Spirit.

Yes, the body has many different parts, not just one part. If the foot says, "I am not a part of the body because I am not a hand," that does not make it any less a part of the body. And if the ear says, "I am not part of the body because I am not an eye," would that make it any less a part of the body? If the whole body were an eye, how would you hear? Or if your whole body were an ear, how would you smell anything? But our bodies have many parts, and God has put each part just where he wants it. How strange a body would be if it had only one part! Yes, there are many parts, but only one body. The eye can never say to the hand, "I don't need you." The head can't say to the feet, "I don't need you."

In fact, some parts of the body that seem weakest and least important are actually the most necessary. And the parts we regard as less honorable are those we clothe with the greatest care. So we carefully protect those parts that should not be seen, while the more honorable parts do not require this special care. So God has put the body together such that extra honor and care are given to those parts that have less dignity. This makes for harmony among the members, so that all the members care for each other. If one part suffers, all the parts suffer with it, and if one part is honored, all the parts are glad.

When I was in the first grade, I saw my teacher Miss White eating dinner at Pietro's Pizza drinking a beer. I was undone! What was she doing out of the school, and why was she drinking a beer? (Never mind the fact that there were two or three pitchers of beer on my family's table.) We like boxes...and we like to put people in them. We like to live in them. We like to put God in them, but He doesn't operate in the confines of "bumper sticker theology." He's fiery and passionate and jealous for our hearts and lives. He longs for us to long for Him, He hates religion (as in man-made rules) and canned spirituality; in fact He came to earth to suffer and die just to break it and set us free. It's time for us to get raw and real with God and take ownership of what He has given us.

If you long for a vanilla life of security and safety with no bumps or bruises, you will also have a safe, vanilla faith with no bumps or bruises. You will probably look good on the outside, but you never really get to experience the depth of the life and love and adventure God has for you. But hey: at least you won't have to risk being talked badly about, right? Having the courage to risk for God doesn't mean we won't feel pain; it means we won't be handicapped by it.

What we do with our talents, gifts, anointing and even our weaknesses speaks to who we say we are and how much we trust Him to deliver what He's promised.

STOP and read Matthew 25:14-30 right now and write down what stands out to you. Take some time to ask God what He wants you to do with it.

{Freedom}
"Your heart is FREE, have the courage to follow it."
-Braveheart

My favorite movie in the history of the universe is *Braveheart*. It's so symbolic of the life of Christ. From a commoner fighting for the freedom of many, to a selfless, sacrificial death at the end. William Wallace fought for the overlooked, he fought for the ordinary, and he fought to set the masses free from the bondage of an evil king.

Wallace's fight was ignited from gut wrenching pain and it ended the same way, quite literally. He started his fight with passion and conviction. That scene where he laid on the cross-shaped table in front of hundreds — in the last seconds of his life as his guts were being ripped out with a hook — told the story of a fearless man finishing with that same passion and conviction. While his executioners taunted him, begging him to say he surrendered, he mustered everything he had, and with one last breath he screamed "FREEDOM!"

I'm a great starter. I start lots of stuff. I may, in fact, have adult onset A.D.D. I like to start new things and move on. I get really excited and sold out on any given project for a few months, and then when it loses its sparkle and easiness, I bail.

|FIGHTING WORDS|: "Now you should finish what you started. Let the eagerness you showed in the beginning be matched now by your giving. Give in proportion to what you have." (2 Corinthians 8:11 NLT).

It's easy to get fired up about a cause when it's glamorous. It's easy to invoke passion and fight in others in the beginning — before the grit of the battle ensues. When we sign up to fight to further His kingdom, there will be gore, there will be baggage and heartache and loss in the course of the fight. That may not speak to some of you. It's hard to willingly move forward when we know there will be adversities ahead. But also know that you're not alone. Soak that in: YOU ARE NOT ALONE and you are stronger than you think.

When I was 30 I hit a wall spiritually. We had lost everything, and I was so mad at God. When I say everything I mean EVERYTHING...our home, our jobs, our savings and most of our pride. As God gently brought me through to the other side, I realized for the first time in my life I had actually encountered Him in a deep way and it changed me.

Since then He's continued to transform who I thought I was and what I thought I wanted in every possible way. I have to admit, with the victory, I have also been attacked on nearly every level. I have lost friends, and the enemy has used people I don't even know to try and stop the work God has started in me. He has used critical spirits, money issues, problems with my children, and personal strife (by a lot of my own doing mind you) to try to derail me.

There are days I felt so weak and wanted to give in; it seemed so much easier before. But I couldn't go back. And neither can you. He has called me, and He has called you, not just to paint our faces and give fancy speeches about the things we're doing in His name. He's called us to be willing to sacrifice everything. He's called us to bare it all in front of the world and scream FREEDOM while our guts are being ripped out with a bloody hook. Um, ok so maybe not that, hahaha, but certainly in the face of adverse Facebook comments or negative words from the world around us. He's inviting us to keep moving forward.

Are you in this for the long haul? Are you ready to love people you don't think deserve to be loved in your life? Are you ready to forgive the unforgivable? Are you ready to surrender everything you think you have a right to? Good, me too, and that my friends is called risk!

FFFFFRRRRREEEEEEEEDDDDOOOMMMMMM!

{Fearless Love}
So I asked my husband to marry me after dating a whopping two months. Nothing about our meeting—or dating or marriage for that matter—has ever been ordinary.

I met C.J. at my senior prom. Oh, he wasn't another student…he was a chaperone. Wait, wait, wait before you get your panties in a bunch hear me out. At my senior prom I saw this straight-laced guy doing his best to bust out 80's dance moves like the "sprinkler" and "driving the bus." (I don't love him for his rhythm.) It was like driving past a wreck; you don't want to look, but you can't look away. *(Just kidding babe, a little.)* Anyway, a group of us surrounded him and started dancing and imitating what appeared to be stepping on a brake pedal. That was it. No introduction, I had no clue who he was. I graduated and worked to save money for a six-month mission trip to Chile, where I blew the little I had saved for college and had to return home to a job at a coffee shop and community college.

One afternoon I was serving coffee to a table of youth leaders from my Campus Life days, and C.J. was sitting with them. Now this was long before Facebook, so when I saw him and felt *that* twinge, I had to stalk him the old fashion way. My friend Stu was almost giddy to be a matchmaker in the process. He leaked the appropriate information to the appropriate sides, and before long I decided to try out the college group C.J. was leading.

Here's the problem: I had been back from Chile for just a few months and was sick of the States already. My friend Michelle and I were on our way to buy plane tickets to Argentina, where we were planning to be freelance missionaries. There aren't enough words to describe how awful our plan was, so I'll just leave it there. The night before the tickets were to be purchased I got her to stalk him up close with me…hmmhmm, I mean…I got her to go to his college group with me. He spoke passionately about the dreams of adventure God had given him and that was it. That night I went home and told my mom I had met the man I was going to marry. No plane tickets were purchased.

After dating for all of two months, we drove to Colorado to meet his family. We were sitting on a four-wheeler eating lunch by the White River on his grandma's property when I asked him: "So, you think we'll get married?"

He choked and then laughed. I was hoping on the way back we could swing by Reno and just seal the deal, but he's a bit more traditional, so four months later, we tied the knot in front of our friends and family.

Sometimes, when God places a dream right in front of us, all we need to do is be bold enough to take the first step toward it. Sure, maybe asking a man to marry you is a bold first step, but I *knew*. And I knew *he* knew. And at that point, it was just about having the guts to be the first to jump. Fourteen years later, one of my favorite parts of our marriage is that we still challenge each other to be bold and move past fear.

What is God asking you to boldly take hold of today? The hardest part is the first step. Ask Him to cover you and then just do it!

{When the Enemy Calls}

Make no mistake, when you move the enemy will move. It might be a subtle deception, or he may come knocking right on your door. In a Circuit Rider podcast talking to a group of students ready to go serve, Brian Brennt said: "You have to be so connected to God that if the devil comes to your door and says 'You'll never end abortion' [because that was the context of their conversation], you'll laugh and say: 'We must be close!'"

I think sometimes when the devil comes to our door we get scared and say, "You're right," and we make our theology match our decision to quit. The enemy is an expert on our fears and weaknesses; he can manipulate any lie into something that sounds like truth and logic. In a film workshop I recently went to, Darren Wilson said, "Fear is the ministry of the devil." Sometimes it's easier to believe his lies than to believe God has something impossibly amazing for us to conquer.

There are times though, when satan's tricks are not so obvious. It's in the quiet before sleep that he sneaks in and mocks us with lines like: "Who do you think you are?" "You're not good enough." "You're not smart enough, you will fail." And while we know those thoughts aren't from God, they can cast a shadow on how bold we are willing to be and what we're willing to risk. Unless we are intimately tied to Jesus, we will let fear, insecurity, baggage, and even the opinion of friends settle us into a life of mediocrity.

The voices in your head—the negative ones--won't die down when you step forward. In fact the bolder and more adventurous you are the louder they get.

I watched the movie *Divergent*, and I kind of loved it. Mostly because the main character just kept doing things that were the opposite of what was expected from her. She was smart and bold and daring, and she asked questions when the people around her seemed content to follow mindlessly. At one point during her testing she had to face her greatest fears; she was forced to enter virtual reality and experience it as if it was actually happening. She was different than the rest of her peers though and was able to come out of the alternate state when she said out loud: "This isn't real."

That was profound to me. How much of what goes on in our heads isn't real?! Those lies, those whispers telling you, "You could never..." *those aren't built on anything real*! What *is* real is a God whose voice roars and thunders with possibility, hope, redemption, adventure and wonder! What *is* real is that you were created to live everyday to its fullest. What *is* real is that He loves you so much He created a destiny only *you* could fill. He created time and space only *you* can affect. He made *you* unique and beautiful and bold and courageous. He made you to be FEARLESS!

{But Even if He Doesn't}

| *FIGHTING WORDS* |*: If we are thrown into the blazing furnace, the God whom we serve is able to save us. He will rescue us from your power, Your Majesty. But even if he doesn't, we want to make it clear to you, Your Majesty,*

that we will never serve your Gods or worship the gold statue you have set up." (Daniel 3:17-18 NLT).

Shadrach, Meshach, and Abednego risked everything with no certainty God would show up and save them. My favorite part of this passage is: "BUT EVEN IF HE DOESN'T." They were so connected to God, they trusted Him so much that they knew even if He doesn't finish their story with the ending they've asked for, God is so good, so mighty and so powerful, that He must have something else for them.

Risk sneaks up on us sometimes. We can be going along, content with the ebbs and flows of life and then BOOM, we have an idea or an opportunity presents itself. Risk is the glue that melds the waiting parts of life to the doing stuff parts of life. And when it pops up in front of you, your insides initially probably do one of two things 1) Scream as you turn and run or 2) Scream as you take off and soar.

In 2010 as we started to settle back into life after disaster, I had an idea. My friend Gena and I started a baby accessory company called Earth Monkeys. We designed three simple products from RPET material, (material made from BPA-free, recycled Coke bottles.) We took months to design a pretty rad bib that we actually even got a patent for.

My favorite thing about the venture was the mom's

blog we created. We just started opening up about the real struggles we faced as moms and wives and developed a platform for other moms to share and be real too. We were inundated with emails from moms saying thank you for dropping the act and for giving them hope. Who knew my inability to filter my thoughts and feelings could actually be a virtue?

We read all the latest marketing books on social media marketing, ordered our first shipment of inventory, got our online shop up, and were ready for the orders to start rolling in. While it wasn't the rush of orders we had expected in the beginning, it wasn't exactly crickets chirping either. But it turns out running a successful business is hard. With five kids between us at the time, what started out as something fun and distracting from poopy diapers and snotty noses took a turn and started feeling heavy and burdensome.

In 2014 we sold the business for what we owed. After trying to balance family and the demands of a business we had both grown less passionate about, we knew we had to make a change. The new owner is awesome and is going to take the business places we never could, but it was hard to admit and own that in the world's eye's we had failed. I'm sure we made mistakes, but we hustled, had a great product and a huge following. Still it just wasn't working for us. I refuse to think of those years as wasted though, because they weren't, I learned so much about relationships, partnerships, and the power of being raw and vulnerable. We risked reputation, money, and time away from our families because Earth Monkeys was something we believed in. We were passionate about promoting the message that moms aren't alone, and it felt awesome that at the end of the day, we were selling eco-friendly products that regular moms like us could afford.

There were losses in that journey, but the journey wasn't a loss. When we were at our wits' end and begging God for wisdom, there was no miraculous Hail Mary pass that pulled us through at the last minute. This venture was the embodiment of "but even if He doesn't." What it birthed in me was even more of a hunger to risk, because after two "failed" business attempts in less than a decade, I knew that even in losing everything, we don't really lose it all. When we can know this deep in our guts, it causes us to take what we can from each experience, reorganize, and ask, "What's next God?" What we gain from each risk may not be material or financial, but it will be life changing if we let it. When we jump off a cliff and say yes to God, we may resurface bruised and banged up a bit, but He always gives us the opportunity to receive gifts in the form of GRIT and GUTS and GUMPTION, and those are things money can't buy.

Do you wish you had the guts to say, "I am going to _____ because God will make it successful"?

(Remember our definition of success may differ from His.) BUT even if He doesn't write the story exactly how I want Him to, it's something He's calling me to and I trust Him!

Take a minute, turn on some music or just sit quietly, whatever floats your boat. Meditate on the words "But even if He doesn't." What does that phrase mean to you?

{Exposed in Front of a Nation.}

When my friend Matt, who had taken over for us at Southern Oregon Sparrow Clubs, called to ask if he could nominate us for ABC's Extreme Makeover Home Edition I was taken back a bit. If we were OK with the nomination, we had to have an entry video shot and created that night. I told him I'd talk to C.J. I made a nice dinner, and by "nice" I mean it wasn't out of can or microwaved, and as we sat down to eat, as nonchalantly as I could, I dropped a teeny line about possibly being nominated for EMHE. Before I could get it out, C.J.'s facial expression was screaming, "No way in Hell."

We were living in a 1950s rundown family rental. We had just barely gotten back on our feet, and the thought of having to expose our heartache, loss, and failure in front of a national audience was not appealing to my hubby at all. Not to mention, we didn't own the property and our house up north that sat on the market for over two years had just sold in a short sale. Credit was not an option. There was no way we could ever buy the property we lived on.

From every angle life screamed: "There is no way you will make the show!" But I still wanted to try. I knew it would be an awesome way to bring some exposure to Sparrow Clubs, and honestly our house was falling apart. All we had to do was take the first step. C.J. agreed to do the video, mostly I think to get me to shut up and really because he didn't think it would ever go anywhere anyway.

As the summer passed, we continued to be blown away as we progressed to each level of the nomination process. But giving producers all of our family info not only felt like a full time job; it was quite invasive as well. They knew everything there was to know about every single part of our immediate and extended family. They knew all of our finances and my children's medical history. It was hugely, let me say it again HUGELY, humbling to expose ourselves on such a raw level after just recently fighting our way back to normal.

At every turn we weighed the risk against the very improbable reward. And every time we came to a challenge we were sure was going to be a deal breaker, God swooped in and just made things happen. We were able to form a partnership and be co-owners of the farm, which in itself was a miracle. And then one day it just happened. Thinking back on it, it feels more like a T.V. show I watched more than a chapter in my life. Sometimes, when I think about how improbable the whole thing was, God reminds me that the wisdom of this world is foolishness to Him (1 Corinthians 3:19).

If we hadn't risked exposing those delicate parts of our lives that hadn't yet healed, we would have missed out on this adventure. If we had reacted out of fear and said no to the first step, we would have been saying no to one of the wildest gifts we could imagine. Sometimes He asks us to risk our things, and sometimes He asks us to risk what people think of us. Sometimes it doesn't turn out how we think, and sometimes it turns out even better.

{True Confessions}

There are a few things that have tripped me up on this road to fearlessness...hmmhmm: *fears* to be exact. When we take stock of our lives and decide to get real with God, we often bring Him our hurt and brokenness to heal and our strengths and gifts to use. I've discovered something I wasn't expecting though; each time I say yes to God, He seems to use parts of me I would have labeled the weakest. He calls out to the parts of me that lies and regret have left frail. Longing to cover up those parts, I question God: "Umm, excuse me God, I don't mean to bother you, but you do realize that part of me you just called forward, it's not really working? It's still a bit bruised, and I'm sure if we put our heads together we can find another part of me that will make you proud." It's then that He gently takes me by the hand, breathes healing into the tender, battered parts and says, "Watch what I can do."

I'm just going to lay it down for you and be real; I have fears, and then I have things I'm terrified of. The contents of the fear list range from awkward silences to frogs and birds; those border on the ridiculous and would never stop me from moving forward. Mostly, they just make me flinch and gag. The list of things that terrify me, on the other hand, are real and born from lies I've believed and dark mocking whispers. Here are my top three:

1) *Being Insignificant:*   I don't know at what age I started fighting against the feeling of being invisible but it has plagued me. Not because I want attention but because feeling significant is directly tied to feeling loved and accepted. Feeling disrespected, and not seen or heard has twisted this fear into all out anger at times.

2) *Being Stupid:* I dropped out of community college because it was too hard. You smarty's out there might be rolling your eyes, but for anyone who has ever struggled with not feeling smart enough you know it can cause some serious damage in the fearless department. When I feel inadequate or don't understand my tendency is to build walls and get

defensive, and to tear down whatever or whoever is making me feel that way.

3) *Being Seen:* "Wait, wait, wait." You say. "Wasn't number one about NOT being seen?" Yeah but fears aren't always rational. I'm afraid of not being seen but probably more afraid of actually being seen for all the parts of me I was never created to be. To have those dark scary whispers I hear at night revealed as truth to you or anyone else... TERRIFYING.

It may seem ridiculous but things I HATE doing the most (because of those before mentioned fears) are; talking on the phone, reading out loud and of course the ever despised public speaking. What I've realized in the past couple of years though is God doesn't just call us to risk in the areas of life that we're good at. He doesn't only ask us to use our strengths and gifts; He delights in taking the most broken pieces of who we are and saying, "Watch what I can do." He does it to me regularly. I hate talking on the phone and reading the Bible out loud, so naturally He led me to start Daily Fighting Words. DFW was a subscription-based service that delivered a daily phone call to your voicemail. For two minutes, I read Scripture and shared a thought or a prayer. (Whew, I got sweaty just typing that sentence!) Every day for six months I had to make a call. It was beautifully terrifying. It was something God used to spark intimacy and depth within His Kingdom, and it's something I would have NEVER EVER NEVER decided to do on my own. After six months of calls, I realized I had the guts of the *Fighting Words Devojournal* I'd wanted to write for years, and it all started with picking up my phone and being OK with the things that scare me.

It's the same thing with those parts of you you're hiding because they have been damaged by years of neglect, lies, and labels. He wants to use those parts because it's in your weakness that His power explodes. That's another one of those verses we've probably known for years, but believing it's true for us is a whole different story.

|FIGHTING WORDS|: Each time he said, "My grace is all you need. My power works best in weakness." (2Corinthians 12:9 NLT).

STOP and ask God how He wants to use the weakest part of who you are to show others how amazing He is!

{Night Witches}

I love true stories of people breaking through social and cultural barriers. The Soviet Air Women of WWII were the first women to be allowed to fly combat missions in the world, and it wasn't without struggle. However, in 1941 when the Nazis invaded the Soviet Union, Stalin caved and approved women to fly in combat.

When the news got out, droves of female pilots volunteered, and three units were formed. These three units of some of the world's bravest women flew over 30,000 combat missions and were a driving force in helping to win the war. The most famous of the three divisions was the 46th. They flew PO-2's: old, slow biplanes made of wood and canvas, used for training and crop dusting. Pilots would idle their engines when they got near their targets and glide to the bomb release point with only the sound of the wind and bombs dropping as evidence they were there. Oh, did I mention they did this at night with no parachutes and only maps and compasses to guide them?

German soldiers named them Night Witches because the sound of the wind swooshing as they delivered their bombs made them think of witches' broomsticks flying through the air. I read that these women were so fierce; any German soldier who shot one down received an iron cross.

In her book, *A Dance With Death*, author and WASP (Women's Air Force Service Pilot) Anne Noggle writes, "Although many of the young Soviet women pilots volunteered as a result of an initial overwhelming surge of patriotism, they quickly came to realize that the war was nothing less than a national life-or-death struggle."

What if, instead of just being fans of our faith, we realized we are in a world-wide life-or-death struggle? God is asking us to live a life of risk and adventure not just for ourselves but for all the other people in our lives who need to be freed from bondage and healed from dark pasts. Your risk-taking breathes courage and life into valleys of dry bones. When you take risks and say yes, no matter what the outcome, people feel freer to do the same. Saying yes to risk is contagious. He made you with lots of guts and more courage than you could ever imagine. He has secret missions He wants to equip you for. Are you ready? Today is the day!

Has God ever asked you to do something CRA-ZAY? Not just a little risky but like gliding a flammable plywood plain into enemy territory at night with no parachute and no compass CRAAAAZY? What did you say?

If you don't think He's ever given you the opportunity to risk big, ask Him to open your eyes to the plans He has for you! And then say yes! Don't turn the page until you've let this sink down into your guts.

Is there something God is moving you toward but you haven't moved on it because you can't see every step?

Is there someone in your life trying to discourage you from following the dreams God has given you? Whatcha gunna do about it?

PRAY WITH ME: Jesus give me fresh eyes and the courage to breakout of ordinary. Lord I'm tired today...physically, emotionally, and spiritually. I am realizing I can do nothing that matters on my own. My attempts to breakout and be different mean nothing and do nothing to further your kingdom. Forgive me. I want You. I want your wisdom and boldness. I want Your love and compassion. Fill me Jesus and push me toward breaking out of this rut. Put a stirring in my guts that can only be quenched by following You. For too long I have been dancing on the edge of the cliff pretending it's the same as jumping, but I want to jump into the unknown and trust You...really trust You like never before. In the name of Jesus, I break off the need for safety. I don't want ordinary any more.

NINE: STRIKE

{Strike a Chord: Breaking Lies on Leadership}
We tend to think of leaders as people who are out in front and in charge, the talkers, the "special people" God has anointed to do…blah, blah, blah!

I look at my four boys and pray daily for God to show them how to be leaders. I don't think any parent looks at their child and says to themselves, "I hope he becomes an excellent follower one day! Lord help him be a wall flower." What a horrible existence! We were made for direct and intimate contact and communication with God. When that happens, an out-pouring of the Holy Spirit inevitably fills our lives. God isn't sitting back hoping we'll blend in and not make waves.

Sometimes we hide behind the line, "Oh, I'm called to serve…behind the scenes. I'm not a leader."

That's a lie. Maybe you are called to serve behind the scenes, but you are a leader in that, so own it. We all have circles of influence: our children, our spouses, our families, friends, and our co-workers. God has given some people large spheres of influence and some smaller. Big or small, they are all important! Some people are called to lead by speaking and teaching out front; some are called to lead by mopping floors and delivering a meal to a sick friend. Our circumstances and backgrounds don't matter. Our jobs, gifts and callings will be different, but all who follow Jesus, are designed to be leaders in love.

How different would this world look if we stopped being passive and started intentionally engaging with God?

STOP believing these hideous lines: "Hey there are leaders and there are followers, we can't all be leaders right? Isn't that what they call too many cooks in the kitchen?"

WRONG, PEOPLE!

It's too many cooks when we are carrying things like pride and self-importance and a need to be applauded, but there is no such thing as too many cooks when we are being fed by the Holy Spirit.

When our message is love and our battle cry is grace,

unity just happens and the Body of Christ moves forward naturally.

We must break the lie of what we "think" leadership is. If you know you're a leader today, I am challenging you to take a real raw look at yourself. Have you been leading with love? Has your motive been to serve God and help others? Has self-importance and the need to be seen doing good ever clouded the once pure vision God has cast for your life? I know I can say yes to that if I'm being honest. It feels gross to admit but we can't overcome what we won't admit.

If you didn't know that you were, in fact, designed to be a leader, I want you to ask yourself why you have chosen to believe that?

I looked up the word "leader" and found two different definitions for the same word. The first one was blatantly "of this world" and sadly has pretty much infiltrated believers everywhere and stunted the growth of the church:

leader
noun
1: chief, head, principal; commander, captain; superior, headman, authority figure; chairman, chairwoman, chairperson, chair; (managing) director, CEO, manager, superintendent, supervisor, overseer, administrator, employer, master, mistress;

president, premier, governor; ruler, monarch, king, queen, sovereign, emperor; informal boss, skipper, number one, numero uno, honcho, sachem, padrone.

And the second one was refreshingly exciting and how I would guess God wants us to see our role in His kingdom:

leader
noun 2: pioneer, front-runner, world leader, world-beater, innovator, trailblazer, groundbreaker, trendsetter, torchbearer, pathfinder. (New Oxford, American Dictionary).

Here's the bottom line:
A good leader values authenticity and transparency over a false sense of perfection.

A good leader says yes to God, even when saying yes means going against the grain of our culture (that includes "Christian culture.")

A good leader doesn't wait until all of her ducks are in a row before moving forward.

A good leader takes the first step out of the boat (or if you're like me, falls butt first out of the boat. Hey, it's still getting out of the boat.)

STOP and take some time and ask God who your circle of influence is. Have you been an influencer for yourself or for God? Have you been too afraid to be an influencer? Ask God what qualifies you to be a leader. The enemy will whisper all of the reasons the world says you're not one. God will whisper, "I am your qualification." Recognize the lies and shut down the accuser; he has no power in your life!

WRITE DOWN the next three steps you need to make to move toward what God is asking you to do.

YOU, my friend, were made to be a leader. You were made for a ministry called life. You were created to love God and His people passionately. When we're willing to place these badges on our lives, when we're willing to tattoo these concepts on our hearts, the earth trembles, and LOVE wins.

{Strike Through Barriers}

|FIGHTING WORDS|: Thus says the Lord of hosts: If you will walk in my ways and keep my charge, then you shall rule my house and have charge of my courts." (Zechariah 3:7 NKJV).

Does it blow your mind that God wants to give us unrestricted access to Him and all He has? We're His heirs, yet a lot of the time, we live like we're orphans. We might know the language and the songs, but a lot of us certainly have not been living like we believe Him. If we did, not one of us would be sitting here unfulfilled, stagnant or bored.

We draw lines. We set up limitations in our heads. We say: "God, I will follow you if... when... until..." We're so conditioned to protecting ourselves, especially if we've had our guts ripped out before, that we draw lines without even knowing it sometimes. Are you ready to go deeper, farther, fuller? I am. Honestly, I'm so sick of being weighed down by the trappings that aren't me.

{Strike into the Unknown}

Not long after we were married, C.J. and I drove to Mexico. We slept in the back of his truck and camped on beaches. It was magical. Before I share this story though, just let me say I know there's an unspoken rule (or maybe it's spoken in some circles) that one should not sleep in one's swimming suit. I ignored it. So one night we were sleeping in the back of the truck all locked in, safe and secure—with all of our gear and clothes outside of the truck, not so safe and secure. That night, I slept in jean capris, a tank and dah, dah, dah...my swimsuit. Though there were about eight bags in our campsite that night, the only two that were stolen were the two with ALL OF MY CLOTHES in them. We're talking no clean undies for over a week, people! It put a serious damper on the rest of our trip. While I was not amused at the time, now I look back and think about how cool it was that we just loaded our truck up and drove through Baja off the beaten path. It was beautiful, and it's only taken fourteen years to be able to laugh about having to wear my swimsuit and my new hubby's undies for a week and a half straight.

C.S. Lewis wrote, "It would seem that our Lord finds our desires not too strong, but too weak. We are halfhearted creatures, fooling about with drink and sex and ambition when infinite joy is offered to us, like an ignorant child who wants to go on making mud pies in a slum because he cannot imagine what is meant by the offer of a holiday at sea. We are far too easily pleased." (The Weight of Glory)

A lot of times when I think of adventure, I think of my early 20's before kids and a mortgage and bills. I think of driving to Mexico on a whim and how I wouldn't even mind having to wear the same swimsuit for eight days if I could just go back and escape life sometimes. I wonder if He's looking at me settling for memories of what once was like those kids making mud pies in the slums. It's only just now occurred to me that He has more adventure waiting for me than I can even fit into one lifetime. What's even clearer is that every time I drop my guard and say yes to Him (even in the boring old everyday things) I'm living a rich adventure. Every time I stop and make time for my elderly neighbor, every time I do something that scares me, every time I forgive, every time I call someone as He sees them, He writes another line of a story marked by courage, boldness and adventure.

Getting to experience His wonder births a hunger for more of Him, and with more of Him comes more opportunities to serve and love and war for others. Wonder really is the birthplace of adventure.

Adventure looks like embracing Jesus' sacrifice and swimming in the power of His resurrection. Did I just lose you? *Ha!* What I mean is: adventure says heaven isn't just waiting for us when we kick it; heaven is *within* us! Heaven is now. When we believe that deep down in our guts, there's nothing we won't do for Him, and there's nowhere we won't follow Him. Your adventure is waiting, what are you going to do about it?

{Strike the Match}
|FIGHTING WORDS|: But if I say I'll never mention the Lord or speak his name, His word burns in my heart like fire. It's like a fire in my bones. I'm worn out trying to hold it in! I can't do it" (Jeremiah 20:9 NLT).

Jeremiah spoke these words in a pit of despair. His friends were turning their backs on him, he was being beaten for the words God had given Him, and he was crying out saying it would have been better that he had never been born, yet even in the depths of his pain he says that God's word is like a fire in his bones and he couldn't keep it in if he tried.

Weston Skaggs has a single called "Fire In My Bones" and the lyrics are chilling:

When the mirror reveals my failures and
Darkness mocks my pain,
When I fall face down in weakness, I remember
You put a fire in my bones.

Whaaattt? Are you kidding me? I love this song so much I had to feed my t-shirt addiction and buy his shirt. As a survivor of losing everything. As someone who can stand up and say I risked and failed. This song spurs me on to claim the truth; victory is knowing and being known by God. He's put a fire deep inside of me that failure can't snuff out and even when the darkness mocks my pain, I can't be silent. I have to move forward, through fear and pain and just dump my baggage. What God has deposited inside of me is stronger than anything the enemy thinks he can take away or destroy! Can I get a hallelujah?

If my friend Mindy's life had a title I think it would be "Fire In My Bones." Her husband, Luke, is a builder, and when the housing market crashed in 2008 they joined us and hundreds of thousands of other Americans who lost everything. This girl is spunky and spicy and anything but ordinary. She's one of my favorites actually.

As a way to make ends meet, she started buying, refinishing, and selling furniture on Craigslist. As her passion and creativity in this growing industry started to explode, God continually gave her opportunities to say yes to Him. "Mindy start a Facebook page. Oh, you're not techno savvy? Don't worry; I'll surround you with people to help you." She said yes. "Mindy start a blog, there are stories I need you to share." She said yes. "Mindy get a booth at the Mercantile." She said yes. "Mindy it's time to open your own store."

This was huge and scary and overwhelming. She and her husband had no money to start a store and no money to stock that store even if they found a way to open it. She prayed and took it step by step: "Lord help us find a building in a prime location that we can afford." He said yes. "Lord help us renovate this old, dilapidated place with no budget." He said yes and without being asked, people started just giving them building materials and décor. "Lord send us people, not just customers, but women who are broken and hurting and don't know where they fit in and let us pray for them and heal them." He said yes. What was once a rundown shop in a dying section of town, now just happens to be in the center of a renovation project the city is investing in to revive downtown Medford.

Mindy and Luke have built their business, Pretty in Paint, into something that is more than a store. They pray for people daily. They have churches and ministries sending women there for prayer and healing. Mindy is bold and passionate about sharing the story God has written in her life. In the face of challenges and a society that says business and faith don't mix, her life screams: "I have a fire in my bones, and I couldn't hold it in if I tried." Mindy's life and success as a business owner are testimonies of what happens when we simply say yes to God.

Mindy says, "Sometimes we think when we do *'that thing'* we won't be scared anymore, and we'll just kind of have arrived. But actually when we do *'that thing'* we're still scared, and God says, 'Are you ready for what's next?'"

Benaiah was King David's head bodyguard. He didn't just wait for life to happen. He chased a lion into a pit on a snowy day (1 Chronicles 11:22). When we live like Benaiah—when we're proactive—God's victory has the chance to shine through fear, doubt, naysayers, and the thought that anything is impossible!

STOP and take stock of what God wants to do in you RIGHT NOW. What dream is burning like fire in your bones? What passion can you not get away from? What is God asking you to say yes to today? Stop and do some journaling.

{Strike the Ax}

You know when you hear something that just changes you? Like the second you hear it, BOOM! You're different and maybe even better. I was listening to Andy Byrd speak once and he was talking about Noah. I obviously knew the story of Noah and how he built the arc, but when I listened to Andy speak, Noah became a real person to me for the first time. He talked about some of the thought processes Noah could have been going through and it absolutely blew me away.

Sometimes when I read through the Bible I honestly don't picture the people with human emotions because they've become so iconic and even a bit robotic to me. But Andy was talking about what it took for Noah to move past human fear, walk out to the forest, and take that first strike of the ax into a tree that he would use to build a boat for God. Noah wasn't a robot. There had to be some hesitation, fear of the unknown, fear of failure. But Noah recognized God's voice because he was in close fellowship with Him. So one day he said yes to God, then he got up out of his seat, grabbed his ax and took the first swing. With that first strike of the ax, Noah was saying, "I might not be able to see the sense in this — it feels overwhelming and impossible — but I trust You are who You say You are."

Some people say it took Noah 60 years to build the Ark, others say 120. Either way, it took decades. Decades of building something that seemed laughable. I imagine those were decades Noah had to stand up to friends and family questioning his sanity: *"Are you sure you actually heard God's voice? Why would he ask you to build this monstrosity in the middle of the desert?"* I imagine fallout and losing friends, I imagine nights of silence wondering if he really did hear God. Of course this is all of my own interjection, pasting my humanity on Noah; maybe it was nothing like that and he really was an obedient, robot of a man who never questioned God when what he was called to do seemed preposterous.

Here's my question: what is keeping you from striking the ax on the preposterous dreams God has given you?

Don't have preposterous dreams? Content with just getting through the day and not eating your boss or children alive? OK, but I have to ask you, is this really the life that you want to live? Today we all have choices, we all have chances, we all have an opportunity to get up out of our chairs, grab the ax and take that first mighty swing, the first strike into what will surely be a life of abundance, adventure, ups and downs, growth and brokenness, victory and triumph. It's risky, though. What if people question you? What if you lose friends? What if what God promises you doesn't happen right away? Ahhh, that's when the real fun begins. That's when we get to not only say the words and sing about trusting God: that's when we get to live it. That's when we get to worship God in the process and realize we carry heaven, (Luke 17:21). That's when we get to embrace the fact that the everyday living and journeying *is* the jewel. That's when we sit and look at all we have, our families and friends our gifts and abilities and praise God that we get to use them EVERYDAY to expand the tent pegs of His Kingdom.

Today, my friend is the day God is calling you to adventure. Today is the day He's beckoning you out of fear and into freedom. It will look different for everyone. For some it's a momentous occasion and for some it's as gentle as a whisper.

|FIGHTING WORDS|: "So he said go forth and stand on the mountain before the Lord." And behold the Lord was passing by! And a great and strong wind was rending the mountains and breaking in pieces the rock before the Lord; but the Lord was not in the wind. And after the wind and earthquake, but the Lord was not in the earthquake. After the earthquake a fire; but the Lord was not in the fire; and after the fire the sound of gentle blowing. When Elijah heard it he wrapped his face in his mantle and went out and stood in the entrance of the cave. And behold, a voice came to him and said, "What are you doing here, Elijah?" (1 Kings 19:11-13 NKJV).

Fear is dispelled and adventure is born when we recognize that sometimes God's voice is a gentle whisper calling us to come to Him. Today He's whispering so intimately to you, "Just come, leave all of the labels and fear and lies behind. You are My beloved, you are My delight. I long for you to just come and be close to Me. Let Me fill you to the point of overflowing with the most radical love the world has ever seen. My Love, My Spirit, My Word will carry you into your destiny and position you to lead others into theirs. You will lead others into knowing who they are and most importantly, knowing who I am. The real Me, not the "Me" religion and humanity have distorted. Will you come? Will you be fearless with Me? Take My hand, let's do it together."

Galatians 5:1 says that it is for freedom that we are set free. You are free today. Say that out loud. I AM FREE TODAY. There is nothing you can't do when you choose to say yes to Him. There is nothing too big, nothing too impossible. You were made for impossible. The world is yours. Fear has nothing on you. You are smart. You are beautiful, and you were created to move mountains!

So I guess we've reached the end of my fearless story for now, but the journey still continues in my life. The question is will you allow it to continue in yours? This past year my husband and I developed a retreat and breakthrough manifesto called STRIKE. As I led the very first group of women through the STRIKE journey, it was amazing to see God work so profoundly. In December forty of us gathered in a rustic lodge in the middle of the Southern Oregon wilderness. Forty women, most of whom hate (hmmhmm HATE) all things having to do with women's retreats or ministry, came together and encountered the power of a God who has designed us to STRIKE past our fears. Everything about that weekend was real and raw and gritty. When it was over, we could have all gone our separate ways, we could be remembering the event tenderly right this second as "that cool retreat I went to once." But what God awakened through the process of STRIKE was too important to become a fond yet powerless memory. Through a secret Facebook group these women have been stitched together in a mighty way. We cheer one another on as we declare the STRIKES God is calling us to and we weep with each other when heart-wrenching prayers are requested.

Why am I telling you this? Because if The Fearless Experiment has unearthed something in you; if any of the words on these pages have awakened parts of you that have long been forgotten, I'm asking you NOT to let the fearless work God wants to do in you end when you close this book.

What if The Fearless Experiment became a movement in your life instead of a book you read once? What if you started your own fearless experiment? What if you dared to take a friend with you?

I don't want this to be the end for you! I want to stand with you, pray for you and cheer you on, through the scary, and through the incredible! So here's what I'm thinking, I want to invite you to begin your fearless journey with me and any other woman brave enough to say, "It's time."

If you're ready to find out who you are and encounter God in a whole new way, email me at lindsay@fearlessexperiment.com, give me your email addy, I'll add you to a secret Fearless Experiment group on Facebook, and we truly will do this thang together!

One more thing though, as you step out, as you say yes to God, as you invite others on the journey with you, document your posts and pictures with #myfearlessexperiment. Because when we tell others about the victory God has in our lives and when we let them see us diving in right where we are; it births a fearless spark in the bottom of their guts too and the enemy loses one more to fearlessness. Are you ready?

PRAY WITH ME: Lord I don't always understand, but I CHOOSE YOU, I relent to you, and I won't fight you anymore. Take me beyond anything I thought possible. Strike through the barriers I've put up to protect my heart and image. Lord, break through the walls I put up, even if they look good. I want what you have to give me. I am ready to be fearless.

Now go out and start your own fearless experiment!

HANG OUT WITH LINDSAY ON...

 www.facebook.com/fearlessexperiment

 @fearlesslindsay

 @fearlesslindsay

 www.pinterest.com/fearlesslindsay

 www.youtube.com/fearlessexperiment

 lindsay@fearlessexperiment.com

 www.fearlessexperiment.com

STAY CONNECTED!
SCAN THIS PUPPY
TO JOIN OUR E-MAIL LIST!

BOOK LINDSAY -OR- C.J. (HER HUNKY MAN) TO SPEAK

ABOUT LINDSAY

Hi I'm Lindsay. I'm a mom of four crazy… I mean wonderful boys. I've been married to my best friend for 14 terribly awesome years. We've been through so much from miscarriages and losing everything, to having two of our four boys diagnosed with autism. What I want you to know more than anything is I'm just a regular girl. My house is messy 80% of the time and clean underwear is a rare commodity around these parts. TMI?? Maybe but I think it's a travesty when women try to put up fronts and pretend we have it all together when we absolutely DO NOT. I love Jesus and I love my family and the rest is just me on a journey with ups and downs, just like you.

In 2011 we received a gift only a couple hundred people in the world have ever received, a home from ABC's Extreme Makeover Home Edition. Since then God has challenged us to open up and get real so that others are freed up to do the same. God has opened our eyes to what it means to truly live, no matter what our circumstances look like. We know that right now, today, God is looking at us and whispering, "If you really believe I am who I say I am, then you have to believe that absolutely NOTHING IS IMPOSSIBLE." I want to help lead believers and non-believers alike to a life of freedom, love and adventure! It won't always look pretty, it won't always feel safe but saying YES to God leads us to depths in our relationship with Him that we never could have dreamed of!

Thanks for letting me be a part of your journey!

Love Your Guts!

REFERENCES

Circuit Riders, 'Kona Podcasts'. *Circuit Riders*. N.p., 2013. Web. Aug. 2013.

Cunningham, Loren, David J Hamilton, and Janice Rogers. *Why Not Women?* Seattle, Wash.: YWAM Pub., 2000. Print.

Goff, Bob. *Love Does*. Nashville: Thomas Nelson, 2012. Print.

Hazlett, Bob. *Roar*. New Haven: Future Coaching Publications, 2013. Print.

Huckberry.com,. 'Attitude Is Everything'. N.p., 2015. Web. 7 Feb. 2015.

Johnson, Bill. 'Weekend Service'. 2014. Presentation. Bethel Church, Redding, CA.

Jones, E. Stanley. *Victorious Living*. New York: The Abingdon Press, 1936. Print.

Lewis, C. S. *The Weight Of Glory*. London: Society for Promoting Christian Knowledge, 1942. Print.

Manning, Brennan. *Abba's Child*. Colorado Springs, Colo.: NavPress, 2002. Print.

Noggle, Anne. *A Dance With Death*. College Station: Texas A & M University Press, 1994. Print.

Stevenson, Angus, and Christine A. Lindberg. 'Leadership'. *New Oxford American Dictionary* 2010:

n. pag. Print.

YouTube, 'The Undoing: Album Promo - Steffany Gretzinger'. N.p., 2015. Web. 7 Feb. 2015.